THE GIFT OF A
PUNISHMENT-FREE
CHILDHOOD

THE GIFT OF A
PUNISHMENT-FREE CHILDHOOD

A NEW WAY TO PARENT
FOR A NEW WORLD

REBECCA WOULFE, PhD

SINGLE LIGHT
PUBLISHING LLC

Cataloging-in-Publication Data is on file at the Library of Congress
BISAC: Family & Relationships / Conflict Resolution

Tradepaper ISBN: 979-8-9888-0190-0
E-Book ISBN: 979-8-9888-0191-7

Cover and interior design:
Victoria Wolf, wolfdesignandmarketing.com.

For all the angels in my life. Thank you.

CONTENTS

PREFACE

LIKE MANY AUTHORS, my goal in writing this book was to change lives. Even if I can improve one child's life, the work will have been worth it. What I discovered in my journey, however, was that punishment-free parenting didn't just change my children's lives; it changed mine. By picking up this book, you are taking the first step in changing many lives—your children's, yours, and perhaps future generations. Punishment-free parenting is different from other parenting approaches in the following ways:

- Parents serve as support to children, not as managers.
- Parents recognize the uniqueness in each child.
- Parents change strategies as children mature and change.
- Parents frame discipline as teaching, rather than as controlling behavior.
- Parents work collaboratively with children to set family expectations.

As you read this list, I hope you feel a sense of relief. You don't have to be an authoritarian, vigilantly trying to control your child's behavior. You can work *with* them rather than against them, hence the unexpected outcome of punishment-free parenting—it opened my heart and allowed me to let down my defenses. Punishment-free parenting truly changed not only my children's experiences of growing up, but it also significantly changed my experience of parenting.

Parenting is a journey. Having raised four children—two with more traditional parenting strategies and two punishment-free—I have experienced both worlds. I can commiserate with you on the daily challenge of getting your toddler dressed and ready for the day, and I can also share the joy of watching your teenager step into a first job or first relationship. *A Punishment-Free Childhood* provides guidance on how to parent across all ages. Beginning your punishment-free parenting journey makes later years easier; however, if you are the parent of a teenager, there is support for you too. It is never too late to change your family dynamics and your relationship with your child. Parents I have worked with have shared about the relief a teenager feels when the conversation shifts away from punishment toward teaching and collaboration.

Parenting matters to me, and as you'll see in the pages of this book, I have uncovered research on the impact of different parenting strategies and the effects of punishment. Over the years, I have also hosted parenting workshops and provided one-on-one guidance to parents. In the chapters ahead, I'll share stories and experiences from my life and other parents' lives to provide you with a variety of resources and ideas. No two parenting journeys are the same. The stories, research, and parenting strategies you'll find here are all resources for you to consider as you begin or continue your journey. I am excited for you to have the opportunity to experience being a parent—it is probably one of the greatest adventures of your life.

So, thank you for picking up this book and being curious enough to explore how you might support your children through a punishment-free approach to parenting. I organized *A Punishment-Free Childhood* in three parts.

"Part I: Parenting Matters" is the *why* of punishment-free parenting. You will learn about how punishment became a part of parenting and some of the negative outcomes that have resulted from its use. Exploring power—how we use it and share it within a family—is also important in understanding the basic concepts of punishment-free parenting. Finally, we'll explore how parents can address hidden hazards frequently experienced by parents: sleeping, eating, mornings, shopping, bedtime, and transitions—opportunities to regularly incorporate punishment-free strategies. This section provides a foundation for your parenting journey.

"Part II: Your Parenting Journey" is the *how-to* section of the book. Chronicled by the developmental stages of childhood and young adulthood, I take you from toddler tantrums through teenage adventures. Parenting approaches need to adapt as children change and develop; therefore, I include a variety of age-appropriate ideas for punishment-free discipline, so you can consider what works best for you and your child. Topics include friends, school, communication, and siblings, to name a few.

"Part III: It Begins with You" provides a chapter just for you, the parent, future parent, or grandparent reading this book. It provides the foundational information necessary for you to care for yourself, so you can be available to your child or grandchild. When you are calm, rested, and self-aware, you will be in a much better place to support your child through behavioral challenges. In the final chapter of the book, I reinforce the importance of punishment-free parenting and how it supports both children and parents. I share the positive outcomes of committing to no more time-outs, no more grounding, and no more removal of privileges. We'll talk about what's next and how your parenting journey never truly ends.

Embarking on this journey to punishment-free parenting took courage. Many nay-sayers thought I was making a big mistake. At each new age, I wondered if it would continue to work. Your journey will also hold doubts, hard days, and naysayers who warn of spoiled children, so I invite you to be courageous. Prioritize your family and your children by using punishment-free parenting. I invite you to step into a new paradigm of parent-child relationships, one of mutual support, love, creativity, and connection. Further, I invite you to find more joy in your parenting journey. Parenting is probably the hardest, yet most rewarding activity, you'll do. Make it meaningful and joyful.

Lastly, I invite you to read this book with an open mind. You don't have to accept all of it; however, I am hopeful that at least some of it will resonate with you. Your relationship with your child, and your child's ability to flourish as an adult, will be all the better for it.

PART I:
PARENTING MATTERS

MOST JOURNEYS START WITH PREPARATION, and this section creates the foundation for your journey into parenting without punishment. In preparing for a trip, you think about what you will take, imagine what your time will be like, and maybe do a little research on your destination. This section provides guidance on how you can prepare for your punishment-free parenting journey. You'll discover how I ended up embarking on this journey and explore *why* punishment-free parenting is important to your family. We'll look at research on punishment and power, detailing the negative outcomes and possible alternatives. You may even uncover the underlying message in this journey: the experience you create for you and your child can have wide reaching ripple effects to effectively change the world. Finally, this section wraps up with a conversation about the challenging parenting situations we address on a daily basis. I call them the Top 5 Parenting Hazards. The ideas in this chapter will lay the groundwork for "Part II: Your Parenting Journey."

I appreciate your willingness to bring me along on *your* parenting journey. As you read "Part I: Parenting Matters," keep an open mind and an open heart. Be willing to think about parenting in new ways and remember that no two journeys are the same. Make your journey your own.

CHAPTER 1:
THE EXPERIMENT

I WAS ENJOYING A BEAUTIFUL SUMMER DAY on the patio with my parents, my brother, and his family, drinking iced tea and watching my two older daughters laugh and splash in the pool. Sarah was a focused twelve-year-old, and Annie was a strong-willed and adventurous nine-year-old. Three years prior, I had remarried and now had two more daughters, Madigan who was just over two years old and Maura who was just four months old. We were having a typical family conversation—what the kids were up to and what movies we had recently watched—when I decided to share my plan with my mother and my brother. I confidently and calmly announced that I was going to raise Madigan and Maura without punishment.

"...punishment doesn't support discipline; punishment teaches people to punish."

I will always remember the incredulous responses of my mother and brother. From the looks on their faces, it was clear they pictured feral children covered in dirt, running through the forest wearing nothing but scant rags. They may have pictured rebellious teenagers talking back to adults and running the streets, leaving mayhem in their wakes. They were nothing short of horrified. I did not let their response change my mind. I knew they were associating punishment with discipline. They could not imagine how you could guide a child and provide the necessary tools for living a healthy and productive life without using punishment. I knew it was an ambitious plan, and I felt some guilt using my own children for a social experiment, but I had to give it a try. Everything I had read, and all of my personal experiences with my first two children, convinced me punishment doesn't support discipline; punishment teaches people to punish.

I went into this experiment a little uncertain. What if I was wrong? What if children *needed* punishment in order to learn and grow? I continually pushed aside my doubts. I worked with my husband to make sure he was on board. He deserves a ton of credit for going along with this idea. It wasn't his idea, and, as he came from a traditional background like me, he had always assumed he would raise his children the way his parents raised him. It didn't take long to persuade him. When he looked back at his childhood and recalled times when his parents had punished him, he only recalled pain, guilt, and shame. Together, we were ready to try a new way to raise our two youngest daughters.

We knew it would be a challenge to change our parenting style to something other than what we knew from our own childhoods. At the very least, we had to become more conscious of our words and actions. Most of what we do day in, day out is unconscious. Think about driving to work. How many times have you arrived at work and had virtually no memory of the trip? Preparing meals, bathing young children, cleaning the house, and even socializing become automatic processes. We know what we need to do and how do it, so we typically find ourselves on autopilot. Changing behavior takes conscious action. It requires being aware of our thoughts, words, and actions. To teach our children about the world without punishment would require commitment.

Some of the changes were straightforward. We made the decision never to spank our children, put them in time-out, ground them, take away enjoyable activities or possessions, or force them to do chores as punishment. At this point, some of you may be siding with my mother and my brother. You may think I am irrational, that I've lost my sanity, or maybe I have just set myself up for the hardest task ever. These thoughts emerge because, at some level, you feel these punishment strategies work, and if I don't use them, I might just find myself with a feral child running through the forest. To your point, these techniques do work. Some of the research I will share throughout this book indicates punishment works really well in the short run, but the use of punishment also has negative long-term consequences that affect not only our children as adults, but also the people around them—their future partners and children.

I decided to launch this experiment after a long journey that included a variety of experiences. First, I already had two children, Sarah and Annie, which meant I had twelve years of parenting and learning under my belt. My greatest take-away was that no two children are alike. Strategies that work for one child may or may not work for another. Parenting is more of an art than it is science. My oldest child, Sarah, served as parenting training wheels for me. I've told her many times she is the one I am always learning from, learning how to care for an infant, then a child, a teenager, and eventually a young adult. I read mainstream parenting books when I was pregnant. I used all of the strategies touted in the 1990s—putting them in time-out, having them go to their room and "think about it," and negotiating rewards and punishment. "If you don't take out the trash, then no video games tonight," or, "If you do five chores this week, then we'll go out for ice cream." Sarah was flexible and understanding and these strategies worked fine for her.

Annie, an exuberant and energetic child, is the person I have learned from the most. Strong willed and persistent, these traditional strategies not only didn't work, but they also backfired. I was at a loss, so I did more research. I found a book with an associated parenting program, *Redirecting Children's Behavior,* by Kathryn Kvols.[1] Kathryn's work made sense to me, and I became a certified parenting course facilitator—sharing her strategies on how to parent. Her work focuses on creating a respectful environment at home. I loved bringing parents together in workshops. I engaged them in exercises—some of which I'll share in here—to help them understand how important it is for children to feel connection and how to provide support when behavior goes awry.

My next takeaway was you can't control the behavior of another person… ever. The more you try to control someone, the more they will resist. I use a simple exercise to demonstrate this response. Put your hand up as though you are going to high five the person next to you, and have them put their hand against yours, palm to palm. Now, start pushing against their hand—what do they instinctively do? They push back. Push your kids, and they'll push back, not because they don't respect you, not because they don't like you, not because they have a defect and not because they are defiant. They push back because it is human nature.

Getting involved with Kathryn's work inspired me to learn more. I found Alfie Kohn, author of *Punished by Rewards.* His work and research demonstrate how rewards (doing five chores means going to get ice cream) backfire. Kohn illustrates how, at home and in the classroom, if we incentivize young people to do things for rewards or to make others happy, they will lose their intrinsic motivation. Each of us acts certain ways for different reasons in different circumstances. I may do the dishes because I like a clean kitchen, and it makes me feel good (intrinsic motivation). However, I may do the dishes because if I don't, my partner gets upset and won't speak to me (extrinsic motivation). Intrinsic motivation is what we want to nourish in our children. External motivation only lasts so long. Alternatively, when a person wants to do something for their own sense of satisfaction, the motivation continues to flow.

MY EARLY JOURNEY BOOKS

Redirecting Children's Behavior: Effective Discipline for Creating Connection and Cooperation by Kathryn Kvols, 2022 revised edition. Kathryn's website: apecparenting.com

Punished by Rewards: The Trouble with Gold Stars, Incentive Plans, A's Praise, and Other Bribes by Alfie Kohn, 1999. Alfie's website: alfiekohn.org

The Secret of Childhood by Maria Montessori, 2009 revised edition. Informational website: amshq.org/About-Montessori/

Finally, the life's work of Maria Montessori influenced my new parenting strategies. I picked up her classic book, *The Secret of Childhood*, in a used bookstore and it instantly touched my heart. She was a wise soul who was way ahead of her time. Her ability to celebrate children, acknowledge their strengths, and understand their perspectives is unmatched. Montessori acknowledges the value of each person and the unique gifts each one brings. She moved education away from a one-size-fits-all structure to a supportive system touting the individual learning process of each child. I used all of these resources to support my parenting style with Annie and they were instrumental in raising an amazing young woman, who, under a different approach, could have become rebellious and been harmed by a controlling parenting style.

My profession also contributes to my interest in parenting and how it not only affects the individual, but also the community. By profession, I am an educator. I have spent most of my career in community colleges, teaching, supporting instructional technology, and serving as an administrator. From this vantage point, I have witnessed great variety in teaching and learning styles. I am intrigued by the learning process, how students learn, how children learn from parents and teachers, and how parents learn from their children. We know children learn the most by watching us, not listening to us. How we act, how we respond, and how we treat them are far more influential than any words we use. Therefore, when I made my commitment to launch my "grand experiment"—raising children without punishment—it was from the position of acknowledging actions over words. If I want them to be emotionally strong, kind, and thoughtful adults, then I would have to *show* them what an emotionally kind and thoughtful adult looked like. My thesis, if you will, was if parents' actions demonstrate adults who use manipulation to get others to do what they want or who use force and power to get their way, then the children will more than likely mirror those traits as adults. Alternatively, if parents' actions reflect a considerate, compassionate, and calm approach, then children will become adults with these traits.

When I looked around the world in 2004, when the two young women who would serve as my test subjects were an infant and toddler, I saw school shootings, a high divorce rate, and violence across the globe, including the 9/11 attacks and the uprising of extreme political groups invoking terrorism and violence. It was time to make a change. My new commitment reminded me of a conversation I had with Kathryn Kvol when she was training some of us to deliver her parenting message. She asked, "When did each of you come to the realization that the only way to change the world is to change the way we parent?" and we each had an answer—because having a positive impact on future generations was why we were there. I wholeheartedly believe each person comes into this world as a representation of perfection. The kind and loving adult, or the cruel and thoughtless one, is shaped through worldly experiences and our innate responses to those experiences.

In this book, I share my experience parenting my first two children using culturally acceptable practices (think of them as the control group in my "grand experiment"). I also share stories from parenting my second two children using punishment-free practices (my experimental group). I include these stories to provide confirmation and give you pause to think about your own life. Throughout the book, I use the singular pronouns "they," "them," or "theirs," rather than "he" or "she." These pronouns are becoming the norm even in academic writing and serve to recognize the fluidity of gender. I believe the use of gender-free pronouns will also improve your experience as the reader as you can replace the generic pronoun with the pronoun of the child you are thinking about. Additionally, if you haven't had children yet, you can imagine the gender of your choice. For readers who are insistent on proper grammar, the use of the traditionally plural pronouns in reference to individuals can initially be disturbing—my apologies to you.

I don't expect you to agree with everything you read, nor did I write this book with the intent to force change. I want you to think critically about the recommendations I provide, but I also encourage you to have an open mind. Many parents fall back on the evidence of their own relative success in life—they turned out just fine given their parents' practices. I challenge you to think not about the status quo, but about a better world, a changed world. Parents hold the future in their hands, and any change has to be made by choice.

I enjoyed sharing a bit about my journey with you in the previous pages. The next two chapters provide additional preparation for your journey— research-backed information to make my case. Once again, I encourage you to have an open mind and heart, recognizing some of this material will resonate with you and some of it will not. Be a sponge, soak it in, hold on to the information you need to guide you in your journey, and release the rest.

CHAPTER 2:

PUNISHMENT'S UGLY SIDE

IN THE PREVIOUS CHAPTER, I told you about some of the experiences leading up to my decision to raise Madigan and Maura without punishment and the books and people who influenced my approach. However, to firmly remove the image of that feral child from my imagination, I had to do a little digging, so I embarked on some research into the topic of punishment. This chapter reveals what I uncovered. We will explore the origins of punishment, how we came to use it as a tool in our society, how we incorporate it into the process of raising children, and finally, the consequences of using it to control the behavior of others. At this point, I want to remind you of my earlier guidance—this book is for you and your journey. If you are ready to dive into actual parenting strategies, jump to the next chapter. If you want to get the foundational information beforehand, stay with me. If you do choose to jump ahead, be sure to come back to this chapter to ensure you have a full picture of this work. This information will help if you start to question whether punishment-free parenting is the right path for you or if you find yourself short on patience and creativity. Being a parent is the most important role you will ever have. It will also probably be one of the most challenging. As this chapter illustrates, the effort is worth the outcome. Not only do you hold the power to create a better life for your children, you also can create a better life for all of us.

"One of the primary reasons for the current use of punishment within families is that the behavior has simply been passed down from generation to generation."

ORIGINS OF PUNISHMENT
Cultural Origins

Punishment has been around as long as humans have been on Earth. However, it is not a part of every culture. The use of physical and psychological punishment varies from society to society, religion to religion, and country to country; some societies have fallen into a greater punishment trap than others. For example, Germany, Spain, Brazil, Ukraine, and New Zealand have full bans on all physical punishment for children, and many others have partial bans. A Nigerian sect refuses to allow any physical punishment of children in their homes or schools. In the United States, we have only just recently banned physical punishment within schools, and we still tolerate it within our homes, although the advocacy I see against it is inspiring. So how did punishment become such an entrenched aspect of our lives, and why must countries have to write laws to end it? One of the primary reasons for the current use of punishment within families is that the behavior has simply been passed down from generation to generation. Individuals whose parents spanked them as a child tend to use physical punishment to control their own children. People who grew up with parents who criticized or humiliated them in order to make them compliant tend to use this kind of psychological punishment on their own children. Many of us have heard the expression, "I was spanked, and I'm okay."

Continuing the practice of physical punishment because it was what you experienced as a child, is not a valid justification. As a human race, we continue to advance and improve the way we do things. For people born in the mid-twentieth century, neither seat belts nor bike helmets were part of their childhood. Many children lost their lives or their mobility in automobile accidents and bike accidents, so we recognized it was time to make a change. Another example is cigarette smoking. Young people once started smoking because it was what their parents did, and it was part of the passage from youth to adulthood. Once scientists and medical professionals learned about the inherent health risks, our society began regulating marketing and initiated educational programs in schools to discourage the use of cigarettes for our youth. As with these and many other examples, using punishment to control the behavior of children is a long-standing strategy not because it is effective, but because it's what we've always done.

Hierarchy and Fear

Research also indicates the more hierarchical a society is, the more likely people will use punishment to control others. For these cultures, punishment is pervasive. Families use it more heavily, criminal justice systems are more punitive, and it is more apparent within relationships. One needs only to think about extremely hierarchical systems like the military, or industrial societies with a need for compliant workers, to get a picture of hierarchy.[2] These systems require compliance and obedience from the vast majority of people and need only a handful of people at the top who are barking orders.

Therefore, the primary goal of the culture is obedience. Children in these environments who think critically or creatively, those who may have a mind of their own, are quickly reined in through physical or psychological punishment to make sure they learn who is boss and who must be obedient, thus further enforcing the hierarchy.

When exploring cultural hierarchy as a source of punishment, it is important to consider the role of fear:

- Fear is a strong motivator, although not necessarily effective or productive.
- Most people fear losing control (remember the wild child running through the jungle).
- Parents may fear losing their position of authority.

People operating from a place of fear resort to strategies based on desperation rather than thoughtfulness and understanding. Fear-filled individuals lack faith in themselves and others and, like a drowning person, will grasp at any and all chances to remain in control, regardless of any negative outcomes. We've all heard the quote, "We have nothing to fear but fear itself." This phrase reinforces the negative consequences we create when we engage with our children and others from a place of fear. Not feeling in control can be challenging for many of us. I know I have experienced fear when letting go of control over a situation or another person, but I have learned how futile it is to grapple for control. It drives you to be more desperate, when all the while it isn't even necessary. In the end, you can't (nor should you want to) control another person, especially when that desire is coming from a place of fear.

Influence of Religion

A section on the origin of punishment wouldn't be complete without a discussion of religious references to punishment. I remember my grandmother saying, "Spare the rod, spoil the child." While this phrase does not actually exist in the Bible, references to a rod and children are present in a few of the psalms. The original Hebrew term translated to "rod" was the word used for a shepherd's staff. The shepherd used the staff to defend the sheep from prey and to guide them toward safety with gentle prods. The shepherd never used the staff as a means to punish the sheep. The shepherd's job was to prevent harm, not cause it. Aside from this common biblical attribution, other religious sects have encouraged the use of physical punishment in raising children. This tie between the origin of punishment and religion more likely stems from the previous concept of maintaining hierarchical power and controlling congregations. In the nineteenth and twentieth centuries, many religious leaders saw themselves as shepherds, superiors to guide and control the herd. Today's variety of religious and spiritual opportunities reflects greater diversity and support for individuals to partake in their own spiritual or religious journey. Many religions are also more democratic, with the people across the congregation engaged in the practice of leadership and worship.

SOCIETAL INFLUENCES

In addition to the practices we picked up from our parents, we are also influenced by the society in which we live. In the U.S. there are many contributing factors to the way we parent and how we incorporate physical and psychological punishment.

"...we are the only country to spend more on prisons than higher education."

Legal System

The U.S. has an overall high use of punishment. We have a high rate of imprisonment compared to other Western countries, and we are the only country to spend more on prisons than higher education.[3] Our political system has contributed to this trend. In the mid-twentieth century, elected officials discovered fighting crime was a proven tactic to gain votes. Candidates pushed for stronger laws, increased prison sentences, and, in some states, reinstated capital punishment. In fact, as other countries were ending capital punishment, the U.S. was restoring it. We also saw younger individuals facing harsher sentences, including imprisonment. In a study conducted in 2000, every state in the U.S. allowed parents to strike their children and held them exempt from assault charges while other countries were institutionalizing no-spanking laws.[4] It is illegal to slap your husband or wife, but we view it as common practice to spank or slap a child. We have anti-bullying regulations in our workplaces and schools, but we view psychological threats as an effective strategy to raise children.

Altruism

Several justifications exist to defend the use of punishment. The first is one I spoke about earlier. There is a fear that lives within us that if we don't discipline our children with punishment, they will grow into nasty teenagers who talk back and run wild. We punish our children in order to save society from their inevitable faults. Some might even describe this as altruistic punishment. Parents justify punishment as the right thing to do because it is what's best for everyone. We've even heard, "This hurts me more than it hurts you," a statement suggesting martyrdom in the practice. Our actions may have a negative impact, but our intentions are good. We are saving the person we are punishing not only from themselves, but we are also saving the rest of the world from the harm this person might inflict. What could be more noble?

Fairness

The second justification for using punishment in our society is the fairness factor. For so long, we have lived by the "eye for an eye" standard of restitution. If you hurt someone, you must be hurt to even the score. If you misbehave or make a mistake, you must suffer negative consequences. Unfortunately, the use of punishment to make someone pay for a crime or misbehavior tends to backfire. Mahatma Gandhi proclaimed that if we follow this approach, we will all end up blind. Individuals sent to prison for minor infractions don't feel remorse; they feel anger and vengefulness. It is a continuous cycle. The punished individual turns around and punishes others in retaliation. Punishment creates more misbehavior, not less. The scope of this book does not cover how to address our criminal justice system. I use it only as an example because, unfortunately, we have taken the concepts of how to manage criminal behavior and applied them to young children who are simply learning how to live in this world.

Retribution

Finally, it is satisfying to rectify a wrong, to use your power to make a point or prove you are right. Spanking and yelling not only serve as punishment, but they are also outlets for our own frustration and anger. The source of this frustration and anger may come as a surprise. When we engage with the people around us, their responses serve to either confirm or deny what we believe. If we believe all children should be seen but not heard, we will feel it is an attack on our belief system when a child speaks out. Is the child really trying to rebel? No. They are simply speaking, but we take it as an assault on our personal beliefs and strike out, not because the child did something wrong, but because of how we interpreted the action. All of this happens in an instant. We are rarely conscious of the complexity of these transactions. Because we feel personally attacked, we feel compelled to defend what we believe to be right. Imagine a trip to the grocery store. We may believe the best way to shop is to get in and out quickly—to be efficient. When a child would rather explore something, engage in conversation, or try to get a little attention during the process, we often lose our patience. How dare they challenge our strategy for getting in and out of the store quickly? This is no time for questions or exploration. Their simple act of asking a question or wanting to look through the toy section feels like an afront. When someone challenges our belief systems, we respond with anger. You have challenged me, so now I must punish you for this wrong, and in punishing, we feel vindicated.

FAMILY INFLUENCES

Because punishment is so pervasive in our culture, it seeps into our families, making the home the most violent setting for the typical American.[5] Stress from unemployment, poverty, relationship issues, and having to care for several children increases the likelihood of physical and psychological punishment within a family. Children whose parents punish them in turn use punishment as a solution with siblings, so violent outbreaks occur between brother and sister. Behind closed doors, it is easy to slip into a vicious cycle of punishment, retaliation, and harm. From a parent to a child, punishment can come not only in the form of spanking, but also in the forms of anger, rejection, negative criticism, insensitivity, and threats. Yelling, insults, and humiliation are all forms of aggression that do not support our goal of raising well-functioning adults. In fact, these actions create a hostile environment where young people fail to thrive.

Several studies on the use of physical punishment indicate nearly all parents hit their toddlers.[6] A very young child is in a powerless position in an extremely hierarchical relationship and has little to no support outside the family. The family is often an isolated unit made up of one or two adults who hold all the power. The adults can give or withhold everything needed to sustain life (food, shelter, love), and they have ultimate authority, especially when the children are young and relatively helpless. A toddler could not survive outside of the family. This is a grim description of a family and is not the only description. Families are also a place of love and joy. A home can be a safe place to learn, grow, and explore, so where does this discussion on punishment fit when we consider our own families? Let's look at the factors influencing punishment within families.

Values

The American family is as diverse as the country itself. We are a country of immigrants and we carry into our modern families the history of our cultures—African American, Spanish, Cuban, Mexican, Asian, Europeans (predominantly Irish, Germans, and Italians), but also many more—too many to list. All of these cultures bring their own values about raising children. For example, Latino families typically value a close family, with each generation supporting the others emotionally and financially. To ensure less independence in hopes of having children stay close to the family to offer this support, parenting styles tend to be more controlling.[7] Alternatively, Western European cultures value independence, so parents are more likely to use suggestions rather than commands when correcting behavior.[8] As we learned in the last sections, different cultures look at punishment in different ways.

Isolation

Another feature of the American family contributing to the use punishment is isolation. Unlike other countries, most families are "single families." We even name our houses as single-family homes. Although great variety exists, the average U.S. household in 2020 had two adults and 1.9 children, down from 2.3 children in 1960. We don't typically live with aunts, uncles, grandparents, or cousins. Most children grow up without several brothers and sisters, a concept which, at one time in history provided a source of comfort and companionship. There are no elders who have lived experience to share. We find ourselves isolated in our homes, doing the best we can with the resources we have on hand. This isolation adds stress to an already stressful life, and we know parents are less patient, creative, and energetic when under stress. All of the attributes we need to support a young child are in short supply. Without a community within the household to help out, we are under greater stress. Rather than tap into alternative ways to discipline and guide our children, it is all too easy to fall back on an instinctual response.

⁓⁓⁓⁓⁓⁓⁓⁓⁓⁓

"We are a fast-food country, leaving work, hitting the drive-through line, and off to soccer practice where we gulp down a cheeseburger and cold soft drink."

⁓⁓⁓⁓⁓⁓⁓⁓⁓⁓

Striving

In addition to stress and isolation, the American family suffers from a sense of urgency. We are a fast-food country, leaving work, hitting the drive-through line, and off to soccer practice where we gulp down a cheeseburger and cold soft drink. Those of us who work often find ourselves driven to move up our career ladders and demonstrate our value as employees. At home, we cram as much fun and housework into our weekends as we can. We are always on the go, striving, and packing in all of life's opportunities as quickly as we can. This insane drive also leaves us with little patience, creativity, and energy. Our lives are rich and full, but at what cost? Our American ideals serve us well in some respects but fail us in others. Raising children is not something we can rush. If you think about when most toddlers throw tantrums, it is usually when they are hungry, tired, or stressed. Often, Mom and Dad feel these same pressures and are also at their worse, creating an environment that leads to poor decisions. To stop the child's behavior and the discomfort for everyone, parents punish the child for their breakdown.

I remember a time when my oldest child was three years old. It was about 1:00 a.m., and she was having trouble sleeping. I was tired, and I knew I would have to get her up and ready early the next day before leaving for work. I was at a loss. I couldn't force her to go to sleep. So, what did I do? I put her in a time-out in the middle night. It was a ludicrous solution. She was sitting in her time-out spot sobbing; I was sitting in another room with my head in my hands. Rather than addressing the issue in front of me, I was thinking ahead regarding what had to be done the next day, feeling a sense of urgency to get her to sleep, so I could go back to bed, and we could rush through another day. Looking back, a better solution would have been to focus on the moment, to consider her needs, find a way to calm her, perhaps hold her until she fell back to sleep, to invest patience and creativity in supporting my child.

Competition

Finally, most American families share America's love for competition. Many sitcom episodes exploit this concept in families competing about the successes (or failures) of their children. To our friends and family members, we tout soccer goals, spelling bee championships, high school GPAs, and college acceptances. We push children to take honors classes and earn college credit before leaving high school. We also sometimes ignore their unique interests because we know what is best and what will get them a college scholarship and a high-paying job upon graduation. For most children, this competitiveness is stifling. When most of us feel stifled, we often revert to lashing out, and our children are no different. They might ignore our requests, stay away from home more, or refuse to comply with our rules. They are exercising their drive to be in control, have their own agency, and follow their own dreams. So, what do we do? We punish them for showing their emotions and asking for help in a negative way. We take away activities they love, threaten to isolate them by grounding them, and may even resort to a slap or a shove. We yell, humiliate, and shame them. We resort to these tactics because by the time they have reached their teenage years, our relationship with our teenager has often eroded and it takes even more extreme punishments to control them.

We have discovered punishment—physical violence, threats, withholding privileges, timeouts—works efficiently in controlling the behavior of someone who is smaller, weaker, or more vulnerable. It is an excellent short-term solution to an immediate problem. When children are young, a swat on the bottom quickly gets their attention. Putting a young child in a timeout immediately stops bad behavior. A slap on the face of a young teenager who is talking back typically astounds them and ends the conversation. Threatening to take away a teenager's cell phone can get them to do just about anything. We use a variety of methods to quickly and efficiently control the situation and the behavior. Punishment is a quick fix.

However, we have also learned punishment has long-term outcomes, and most are not so positive; our quick fix is also a quiet destroyer. The next section goes into more detail on the consequences of using punishment. Our children learn what they live (not necessarily what we tell them), and with our shortsighted approach to discipline, we teach them punishment is the solution.

NEGATIVE CONSEQUENCES

Before we dive into the negative consequences of using physical and psychological punishment, I want you to take a minute or two to explore the "Personal Experience Exercise" provided.

PERSONAL EXPERIENCE EXERCISE

Close your eyes and think back to a time when someone punished you as a child or teenager. Consider the following:

- What did you do, and what were the circumstances?
- Who punished you?
- How did they punish you?

After recalling the experience, answer the following questions:

- How did you feel about the situation?
- Were your feelings positive or negative?
- Were you motivated to change your behavior?
- How did you feel about the person who punished you?

This exercise gives you the opportunity to recall the perspective of your childhood self and can inform us regarding how most children feel when punished. I imagine the punishment you recalled left you feeling angry, hurt, or frustrated, rather than willing to comply next time. The research on punishment supports your experience. Punishment:

- Doesn't result in long-term behavior change.
- Damages relationships.
- Often leads to more aggression.

Ineffective

Based on your own response to the previous exercise, it should come as no surprise to learn that when a researcher asked parents if they had previously punished a child for the same behavior, 73% of the time they said "yes."[9] If punishment worked, it would end the bad behaviors, but it doesn't. I remember my own disbelief when I learned, "punishment and misbehavior are part of the same cycle."[10] Wait a minute! I'm trying to stop misbehavior, and you're telling me I'm only causing more? It was a turning point for me. My mother once described to me a situation with her friend's highly energetic young son. The parent was distraught and could not get her child to obey. My mother uttered the words, "The more she tries to control him, the worse he gets!" She made this statement out of frustration, but I heard it as a solution. If the parent curtailed her efforts to control her child, the child would not feel so compelled to act out. This example supported what I had read about misbehavior and punishment being two sides of the same coin. When you recall your punishment story, did you feel remorseful, obedient, and positive toward your punisher?

> "Teenagers, in particular, are often the recipients of relationship damaging punishment."

Damages Relationships

This leads to another consequence worth exploring. What happens to the parent-child relationship? If many of the interactions you have with your child are about proving to them who is in charge and showing who sets the rules and divvies out the punishment (and rewards), you may want to reconsider. If you suggest you are above them, a superior who vigilantly watches for any step outside your set boundaries, your child may not be so keen on spending time with you. In fact, they may actually try to avoid you, which, of course, you will then perceive as misbehavior. Alfie Kohn describes how when a child acts out, we feel as if "our authority has been challenged, and the more we construe a relationship as a battle for power, the more wildly we will lash out to preserve that power."[11] Our relationship shifts from one of support and guidance to help our child become a confident and independent adult, to a relationship comprised primarily of power struggles which serve neither the parent nor the child. A child begins to dread your presence if your primary role is to reprimand and deliver punishment.

Teenagers, in particular, are often the recipients of relationship damaging punishment. Because they are bigger and stronger, parents can no longer use physical coercion to control their behavior, so the psychological tactics begin. Remember the exercise we did at the beginning of this section? As I describe some of these punishments, picture yourself as the teenager, not the parent. A parent shared with me her story of how she controlled her daughter. If her daughter took a shower for over ten minutes, she would turn off the hot water. This action was telling her daughter, "I love you, but I'm in control of how long you can shower and will make sure you suffer if you exceed that time." A teenager who arrived home thirty minutes late had her keys taken away for a week. "I love you, but you will absolutely abide by my time clock." Grades in school can also be a source of contention, so it comes as no surprise when teenagers simply give up. A teenager gets a B in Algebra rather than an A, so they have to give up frisbee golf until their grades improve. "I love you, but you will get the grades I want you to get and because I know you so well, I can take away the one thing you love the most to get what I want." If you have been imagining these examples through the eyes of the teenager, how are you feeling now? What have you learned? How do you feel about your parent?

Leads to Aggression

Punishment is not as effective as we think it is, and its use contributes to the erosion of our relationships. However, what is even more concerning are the long-term consequences. Research over the last several decades has confirmed punishment results in aggressive and punishing behavior. The child who experiences consistent and violent punishment becomes the domestic abuser. Violence encourages violence, and punishment encourages punishment. A child who is spanked is twice as likely to physically attack another child.[12] If you consider the practice of using punishment logically, these results make sense. When parents use aggressive forms of discipline, children model their aggression.[13] Remember, children learn what they live, not what we tell them. If it weren't so destructive, you could see the irony of a mother shouting, "Stop hitting your brother," while spanking the offending child. This ludicrous example shows the kind of mixed messages we send our children with the use of punishment. It's okay to hit if you are in a position of power, if you are the boss, or if it serves you. You can easily see the message a child internalizes.

All the negative consequences shared in this chapter were the motivation for my experiment. They were the reasons I had to see if I could raise children without punishment. I could see a common underlying theme in much of the destruction I witnessed in the world. The Columbine High School shooting in 1999 illustrates this theme. The shooters wanted their schoolmates to suffer; they wanted to punish them for their acts of hazing and ridicule. The horrific events of the 9/11 attack are another example. The attackers felt justified in their actions because they needed to punish Americans for their capitalistic, ingenuine, and secular way of living. If we could end or even mitigate the need to punish, we could start to shift this trend. If children didn't learn to use punishment as a solution, then maybe we would see less destruction in the world around us.

I'll close with some research data[14] to support my hypothesis. In countries that have made spanking and all forms of physical punishment illegal for parents, they have seen:

- 80% reduction in juvenile delinquency.
- 68% reduction in domestic violence.
- 46% reduction in serious depression.

If a reduction in domestic violence means your daughter or son will be able to live in a healthy relationship without the threat of violence, don't you think it might be worth it to see if we can make a difference? We can change our behavior to encourage supportive relationships rather than adversarial ones. It's time.

Thank you for taking the time to explore the ugly side of punishment. You can recall this information when you are wondering if punishment-free parenting is worth it. You can remind yourself of the importance of this work when colleagues, family, and friends question your approach. You can feel satisfaction seeing the positive results in your relationships when you consistently parent without punishment. The next chapter continues to set the foundation for punishment-free parenting by addressing the topic of power within families. Power is a complex subject, to be sure, but it is an important one as we look at how to support our children in becoming loving, conscious, and joyful adults.

CHAPTER 3:
WHO HOLDS THE POWER?

PUNISHMENT'S SIDEKICK IS POWER, so a discussion on punishment-free parenting wouldn't be complete without acknowledging the role of power in families. Power is prevalent in our lives, and it both serves us and hinders us. To better understand the power dynamics of punishment-free parenting, I did some additional research. To bring your best self to this parenting journey, you need to understand how power is at play in our families, how we use it, and how we abuse it. In this chapter, the first area we'll explore is power dynamics in families. Who holds the power? How is power used? How do we empower children? After a little background, I will outline approaches on how to distribute power equitably within the family. To create healthy and confident adults, it is important for parents to support and empower their children. This chapter gives you three tools to succeed with this mission: giving children choices, allowing for their voices, and providing opportunities for them to be experts. Before diving in, take a few minutes to read the story I crafted, "The Enlightened Princess."

THE ENLIGHTENED PRINCESS

Once upon a time, a beautiful princess lived in a tall tower. She had everything she wanted or dreamed of, surrounded by luxury and beauty. On one particularly beautiful morning, when the sun was shining, the flowers were blooming, and the grass was green and glistening with the morning dew, the Princess decided to go for a walk. She began in the castle gardens where the flowers were beautiful and the hedges were manicured. She was feeling full of life and courage, so she began to wander past the confines of the castle grounds. As she walked toward the city, the landscape began to change. Litter replaced the flowers, rough cobblestones covered the green grass, and buildings blocked the sun. Wishing to go unrecognized, she pulled her cloak tightly around her and covered her face. Of course, this strategy did not work. The finery of her clothes, shoes, and cloak, even her own cleanliness, gave her away. A small child in ragged clothes, walked up to her. "Miss! Miss!" he cried as he held up his empty tin cup. She turned to look at him, and, in his eyes, she saw her own. Behind the grime and the ragged clothes, she saw his youthful and passionate spirit. She shared a few coins with him, and he ran off to get food to share with the other children on the street. It would be a good day for them.

As the princess began her return trip to the tower, she viewed the luxury of the castle with new eyes. In her heart, she now knew there were no differences in spirit, yet, she had witnessed a disparaging gap between those who rule and those who are ruled. She knew her life had changed forever. When she stepped into her role as queen, she would pronounce a change. She would find ways to provide food and fresh water for the townspeople. She would ensure the streets were clean and lined with flowers. She knew these gifts would come with a small price, yet they would enrich her life because the lives of those around her would also be richer.

What does this story have to do with power in our families? It demonstrates how sharing power doesn't disempower adults. Ensuring children have opportunities to learn about power and feel powerful is important. The story also shows how we are all part of a larger community—those with wealth and power and those without. In our homes, we can choose to be part of a small community that thrives and lives in harmony, or we can be part of a community of kings and peasants—those who hold the power and those who don't, as well as those who can ask for what they want and those who cannot.

The power dynamics in a family are complex. Adults bring life experience, knowledge, an ability to create a natural rhythm to the day, and a focus on safety. Children bring life, love, curiosity, naiveté, and a focus on exploration and learning. Sometimes, these differences are honored and supported, creating an environment in which everyone can learn and grow. Other times, these differences represent dissimilar degrees of value, creating homes full of adversity, frustration, and sometimes, anger. Additionally, the size and strength of the individuals within a family contribute to power dynamics. Adults are larger and can physically overpower children. Adults also provide the necessary resources to sustain life—food, water, and shelter—and they have the power to withhold these resources. So many components are at play when we consider power dynamics in families. However, when one side of the power equation becomes too dominant, the whole family feels out of balance.

I saw power dynamics play out when our family made a trip to Yellowstone before my "experimental" children were born. Because my husband and I were responsible for the children staying safe and together, the power dynamic shifted toward us, the parents. We were diligent and hypervigilant in ensuring everyone stayed together. If one of the kids started to wander, our senses became heightened, and at one point, I watched my husband exert physical pressure on our child to bring her closer, holding her hand with extra firmness. Our children, on the other hand, were in a new space—a national park with a lot to see. They wanted to explore, play, enjoy, and experience this new and interesting environment. You can see how our energies were at odds—not only different but actively clashing. It didn't feel good, and something in me stirred. There had to be a better way.

"Life is too short, and my relationships with my children were too important to spend every morning arguing and fighting."

As with the pushing hands exercise, I learned that the more we, as parents, try to control or exercise our power, the more the children say no and push back, wanting to exercise their power to run, play, and explore. The situation often ends with tears, anger, and frustration. In our case, a delightful young teenager turned sullen and moody. You might be thinking of your own experiences when your intentions may have been good, but the situations spiraled. Perhaps a fight about when to eat or what to wear. During conflict, parents tend to blame children, and children—especially teenagers—tend to blame parents. However, it isn't anyone's fault; it's simply two different approaches or two different perspectives.

Power struggles can sometimes be part of daily rituals. When I was a new parent, I remember mornings as being especially hard. Once again, my focus and needs were very different from the needs of my young children. I needed to get to work on time, so my focus was on efficiency—getting myself out of bed and getting my two children up, fed, dressed, and out the door in a specific amount of time. However, young children have a different focus. Their bodies are growing and have irregular and ever-changing needs. They have spurts when they eat everything in sight, and they also go through phases when they eat very little. They have days when they have high energy and days when they need a little extra sleep and rest. Their body rhythms are part of a natural cycle; they are not a rigid schedule dictated by a clock. I think you are starting to get the picture. Parents have more precise and regular timing, whereas children have more natural and fluid timing. The two are quite different, hence the morning drama.

I began to explore new parenting options because of the morning challenges I was experiencing at the time, but I also uncovered some basic parenting tips. Life is too short, and my relationships with my children were too important to spend every morning arguing and fighting. The first strategy I uncovered was to lower my expectations. Did it really matter if a three-year-old's top and pants matched? Would the world end if my child went to pre-school in their pajamas and opted for regular clothes a little later in the day? After recognizing how chasing perfection—or anything close to perfection—was causing strife, I let go. I started to give my children a *lot* of choices. In other words, I started to give them power in the relationship.

If you think about power dynamics in a family, the odds are often against the children because of their smaller size and lesser strength. Though I learned rather early on that you can't force a child to go to sleep, you *can* force them to do many other things, such as get in the car, get back into bed, and, sometimes, stay quiet. Adults also have more language ability and experience. Children are small and lack some skills, but they are still human and are still driven by the same general motivations as adults. They want to have a say in their lives, and they want to feel empowered and valued. The more everyone in the family feels that they have a voice, the more likely peace will reign over adversity.

A CHOICE IN THE MATTER

As I watch my children grow and become young adults, I continue to see the importance of choice. Each of us makes choices every day. There are small choices such as what to wear, whether or not to exercise, and when to speak up; and there are also big choices such as where to attend college (or whether college is the right path), who to marry, and where to live. The more opportunities we provide to our children to make choices when they are young, the better prepared they will be for the big decisions when they become adults. If we make all of the choices for our children, we will continue to finesse our own abilities, while they will face future struggles.

For some people, the thought of letting children make their own choices causes them to feel fear. If you are feeling afraid, stop to ask yourself why. Many parents I work with have shared concerns related to giving their children the freedom to make choices. What if the child makes the wrong choice? What if other people don't approve of my child's choice or don't approve of me giving them a choice? What if there are long-term negative consequences? What if my children don't need me as much if they are able to make their own choices? These examples represent only a few parental fears, and if there is one thing most parents are good at, it's finding ways to be fearful about their children. Let's look at these fears, tease them apart, and explore a way forward.

Fear of Bad Choices

So what if your child makes the wrong choice? First, I want you to recall how you are the one who brings experience to the situation. You have the ability to determine which choices your child is ready to make and which choices will require your additional guidance. As with most strategies, it is important to consider the developmental stage of your child. I remember learning that a child under the age of five is unable to distinguish the concept of telling the truth versus the concept of lying. To tell a three-year-old not to lie is a waste of breath. Their brains have not yet advanced enough to understand the concept of a lie. Determining whether to let your child choose requires an assessment of their developmental stage.

For example, would you let your young child decide what to have for dinner every night of the week? If you did, you would likely have to live on a diet of pizza and hamburgers. You can, however, allow them to decide what to have for dinner every Tuesday night, or you could let them choose which of three vegetables would go well with the dinner you are already preparing. When it comes to clothes, your child is capable of deciding what to wear to go to the park, but they may need your help for an important event, such as a wedding or a graduation. Remember, children are like us. When we have a part in making decisions, we will be more likely to engage positively with the activity.

Fear of Disapproval

The fear of disapproval from others seeps into our lives in a variety of ways. How we raise our children is an area where we often feel this external judgment. Determining how you want to raise your children is a personal choice. As with all differences, some people will appreciate your direction and others will disagree. To mitigate the fear of disapproval, think back to other times in your life when you moved forward with confidence, despite knowing not everyone may necessarily agree with you. Recall how it felt to be courageous and to follow through on a decision that was right for you. Regardless of the direction you take with your children, dissenters and supporters will provide their opinions for either side. Look for the supporters, build your community with like-minded individuals, and let others have their own journey without your judgment.

Fear of Hardship

We all want our children to be happy and avoid pain and hardship. How many times have we wished we could spare our child from an illness or a fight with a friend? The fear of negative consequences—especially long-term ones—from choices we let our children make is very real. However, the alternative to preventing them from making these choices is more dire. If we sacrifice children's opportunities to learn how to make their own decisions, we set them up for even greater challenges and possible threats when they are teenagers and young adults. Your goal is to prepare your child for living and making decisions outside of your home. They need to have had experience making choices—suffering from poor ones and thriving from good ones—while you can still offer support and encouragement. If the first time they must make a choice is when they are at a party with friends and you are not there, they will struggle and will perhaps make a poor choice.

Fear of Not Being Needed

The fear of not being needed is the final fear I'll address. For many parents, their relationship with their child is one of the closest relationships in their lives. A component of this closeness is the sense of unwavering support. Knowing you are contributing to and improving someone's life with your support, gifts, and guidance feels good. It is hard to imagine your relationship with your children without this sense of being needed. In many cases, we fear we may lose the entire relationship if our child no longer needs us. For those of you for whom this fear is very real, I would suggest your relationship with your child will be richer, stronger, and healthier when it is balanced. When your child and you both feel important and competent, the relationship is stronger. When your child becomes an adult and reciprocates your care, support, and gifts, you will experience even more closeness. If you do your job well, your child will grow into a confident and caring adult. Your relationship will change over time. It is a natural and quick shift when you go from caring for an infant to caring for a toddler then to caring for a young child. Most of us are pretty happy to be done with the diaper bag! The same is true for other transitions. They don't lead to loss; they lead to the next stage of your parent-child relationship. Now, let's take a look at how to implement opportunities for choice.

OPPORTUNITIES FOR CHOICE
Young Children

Age-appropriate choices are important, and young children need plenty of practice. Examples for young children, three to five years old:

- Of the three outfits on the bed, what do they want to wear today?
- From the bookshelf, which book do they want to read tonight?
- Which side of the back seat do they want to have their car seat buckled into?
- Do they want dessert after dinner or after pajamas?

As you can see from these examples, choices help young children feel as though they have some say in areas where they still may need your guidance. Giving children choices can eliminate the need for punishment and threatening language. Rather than get into a power struggle with your child or have the need to overpower them, give them a choice.

Older Children

For children who are a little older, ages six to ten years old, you can begin to give them more important choices. At this age, they are learning about friendship and are usually engaged in activities outside the house such as sports, dance, or music lessons. They are also ready to start contributing to housework and yardwork. All of these situations provide opportunities to support them in making decisions. When they want to go to a friend's house, rather than dictate a time, have a conversation with them. You can ask questions such as how much time they think they will want to spend at their friend's house or if they will be comfortable eating over there. You can then share your needs and experiences as well. Share your schedule and provide good times for you to drop them off and pick them up, including more than one, so they have options available. Through a conversation, the two of you can determine what will work best for the playdate.

This is also an age when you can let them decide what to wear. Let them have a voice in what clothes to buy when shopping. Set a financial limit and let them select what they want. They will learn that it is sometimes better to spend all their money on the great coat they really want, and it is sometimes better to bargain shop because they need several pairs of new pants. When you give them the opportunity to learn these lessons while they are young and under your supportive wing, it means they won't have to learn them when the consequences are higher.

Your home is a safe place to learn and grow. If you make all of the choices, dictating what your child wears, who they play with, and what they eat, they will have limited experience and will stumble more when they leave the safety of your home. Does this mean you never provide input? Of course not! When it's time for Aunt Suzy's wedding, your input will be important. We had a saying in our house when we were going someplace a little nicer, "No stains. No holes," and everyone knew they had to select clothes to wear to fit the occasion. Michelle Obama, in her book *Becoming*, shares the story of her own mother who always said, "I'm not raising babies. I'm raising adults."[15] To raise an adult, you need to provide your children with the opportunity to test out adult-like decisions at an age-appropriate level.

MISTAKES

When a child makes a mistake, it is not the time for reprimands or "I told you so's." It is a time to offer support. Children fare better when they know you are on their side and will support them when they need help. An example many of us have experienced is when a child forgets an important item at home that they need for school. One approach is the consequences strategy. You refuse to take it to them, so they suffer the consequence of their forgetfulness. This approach compounds the child's pain and frustration. They don't have the item they need for school, and they feel alone in the world. The alternative is for you to take it to them and let them know we all make mistakes. They learn this is a caring world, we all are fallible, and it is okay to ask for help. Now, situations do occur when you can't take the forgotten item to them because you have a commitment. The difference is in the message. You can say, "It's your fault you forgot it, so you will just have to do without," or, you can say, "Everyone forgets things every now and then. I can't bring it to you today because of my meeting. Talk to your teacher and ask what you can do." This way, your child will learn rather than feel punished.

Outside of clothes and playdates, keep food choices in mind. Educate your children about nutrition. Together, decide how many sweets and salty snacks make sense in a given week and let your child decide when they want to have them. The best way to learn about overeating is to overeat. The best way to learn about the effects of too much sugar is to experience the outcome. Remember, this is when we want them to make mistakes—when we are here to support them and the best way to learn about eating well is to feel what it is like to eat well.

Teenagers

Now we have come to the age when allowing your children to make choices becomes harder because the stakes are higher. Teenagers. The ages between twelve years old and sixteen years old are often referred to as challenging years. Children are stepping out on their own, testing boundaries, learning to drive, and spending more time with friends. These years will be easier if you have spent the previous years giving your children ample opportunities to make choices and mistakes, thereby learning from them. They will now be confident and assured, and will not feel the need to rebel. Nothing exists for them to push back against, because you have not been pushing, nor have you been trying to control them. You have let them grow, learn, and become unique individuals with strengths, passions, and gifts of their own. As an example, I have a memory of when one of my younger daughters started to date. She was going out on a week night, and she opened the conversation with, "What time do I need to be home?" to which I responded, "Well, you have school tomorrow and don't want to be too tired. What do you think?" She asked, "Would 10:30 work?" and I said, "What about 10:00 since that's when we go to bed, and I can still be up when you get home." She agreed and was willingly home by 10:00. Teenagers who have a say in their boundaries are much more likely to stick to them.

"Giving your teenager choices does not mean they run through the forest in ragged clothes with no boundaries."

This example brings up a necessary conversation about choices. Giving your teenager choices does not mean they run through the forest in ragged clothes with no boundaries. All of us need boundaries—the incentive to come to work on time, pay our taxes, or drive safely. The same is true with children. I didn't tell my daughter she could come home whenever she wanted. Rather than having no boundaries, we worked together to decide what suited everyone involved. Teenagers, as with adults, sometimes end up in situations when they can't get home on time. Think of a time in your own life when a meeting ran long, and you had to let your colleagues in the next meeting know you would be late, or a flight was delayed, or an accident occurred on the freeway, or your car wouldn't start. Life is full of inconveniences that can cause us to miss a time commitment. The same is true for everyone, even teenagers. I have often thought it is unreasonable to hold teenagers to a higher standard of punctuality, when they don't have the resources nor the experience of an older adult. When they are late, miss a curfew, or oversleep, they are often met with punishment or are labeled lazy. Our experiences are different. We typically receive compassion or understanding if something goes awry in our lives. I expect my children will run into issues too. I tell them to call me if they are running late. I remind them they won't be in trouble, but it is also important to keep me informed.

To go further with this idea of parents being a safety net, my husband and I made a pact with our teenagers. If they found themselves in a situation where they didn't feel comfortable with their original plan for getting home, they could call us, no questions asked, and we'd even throw in some cash. No circumstance was too extreme. They could call us if they drank too much, if their date had drunk too much, or if their friends wanted to do something that didn't feel right. We wanted them to feel comfortable calling, even if they had made a mistake or had ended up in a bad situation. They needed to know we were their safety net, not their judge and jury. So far, we have only had one child take us up on the offer, and I can tell you, as a parent, I have never been so relieved. It is so much better to get the call from your child saying, "Mom, I don't think I should be driving. Can you please come get me?" rather than one from the state patrol informing you of an accident.

What kind of decisions can your teenagers make? By now, if you have created a safe environment for your children and have given them plenty of opportunities to make choices while growing up, you will be able let them make most decisions. They can certainly make decisions regarding what they wear and how to manage their time and money. Again, this is the time for them to make mistakes with money, when the stakes are not high, when you are still there to provide necessities if they have squandered their money. If you manage their money for them now, those same mistakes could be much more costly once they go out into the world. As described with my last example, we collaborated with our children on curfews, ensuring everyone was comfortable. We also let them manage their schoolwork. We did not look up their grades each night to see what assignments were missing or if a class grade was not high enough. Those grades belonged to them, and they knew they were responsible for them. We were not absent from the conversation, but our input came through modeling the importance of education. We had conversations about what kind of grades it took to get into different colleges and universities. We talked about dreams, hopes, and desires. In the end, all of our children were responsible for their own grades, and because they owned them, they did well.

As teenagers transition into young adults, they will more than likely be thinking about what happens after high school. Do they want to go to a four-year university? A community college? Enter the work force? This is a time when it can be challenging not to force your ideas of success and happiness onto your children. You may have always thought your son should be an engineer, but his heart is in the arts. Support him in following his passion. His dream will guide him to his success. No two paths are the same, and no degree or job can guarantee success. If you force him into an engineering pathway, he would eventually be unhappy and need to make a change later in life, when it is often more challenging. As a parent, it can be hard to trust in your young adult, but trust you must. You have given them ample opportunities to make choices and to learn from them; they are ready to spread their wings.

I have one final word on choices. Choices should always be positive. I have heard parents use the idea of choice to control a situation by asking, "Do you want to go to bed on time so you can play your video games tomorrow, or do you want to stay up late and lose your video game privileges?" Choices with punishments built in are not true choices; they are threats disguised as choice— wolves in sheep clothing. You want to support your child in becoming a competent adult by teaching them to make choices, not manipulating choices to control them.

Think back to a time when you were young and in the moment. You may have been playing with a friend in a sandbox or alone with a book. Do you remember the feeling of being absolutely engaged with life? Did you feel frail and incompetent, or did you feel strong and confident? We need to remember our children, even at very young ages, do not feel weak and in need of protection. They feel strong, capable, and energized. Support them in stepping into their strengths, exercising their competence, and pursuing their passions. Let them make a lot of their own choices, so they can fully express their abilities.

A VOICE AT THE TABLE

I remember a visit with my sister-in-law when her oldest child was about thirteen-years-old. About five or six adults were sitting around the big dining table drinking coffee. He came in and sat down, and we asked him the usual questions about school, sports, and friends. Instead of getting up to go back to being a thirteen-year-old, he stayed, adding his opinion and sharing information. He was testing out his voice by contributing to the conversation. It was awkward, and he said a few things that didn't really fit with the topic, but I knew, even then, the importance of letting him have that practice. My discomfort over some of his awkward responses was insignificant compared to the importance of allowing a young person in our family to step into conversations with adults and have a voice.

When someone has a voice—being able to share their opinion and agree or disagree with the people around them—they have a sense of agency. Agency means we are able to confidently and independently carry out our ideas and plans. Most of us have a sense of agency in many areas of our lives. We are capable at work, we can make decisions at home to keep the household running relatively smoothly, or we may be active in our community or involved in politics. Adults demonstrate agency in many ways, and it is an important strength to instill in our children. Remember, we are raising adults, not babies.

During my time researching power within families, I came across Albert Bandura. Many researchers consider him to be the expert on the study of agency and its importance in our lives, specifically the need for individuals to feel they can be effective. Bandura suggests that unless people believe they have the ability to impact their environments with their voice and actions, they will have "little incentive to persevere in the face of difficulties."[16] With a strong sense of agency, children are successful in school, more resilient in the face of challenges, and stronger in their morals. Individuals who feel effective and capable are less vulnerable to depression and stress, and they have a more optimistic outlook on life. It is important to nurture this sense of agency by giving children opportunities to stretch their abilities, have a voice, and feel a sense of accomplishment as they mature and develop.

Opinions

What are some ways to give our children a voice? How can we support them in feeling empowered, acting with agency, and positively affecting their surroundings? We will want to make sure our guidance is age appropriate, and our children are developmentally able to contribute. When children first learn to talk, it is already time to start asking them their opinions. For example, when shopping for food, have them taste a raspberry and a blackberry and ask which they like better, or ask them to identify which one is sweeter. At the dinner table, ask them about their day. What was the best thing that happened? What was the worst thing? Children need to learn early on how to talk about negative experiences and to realize we all have them, so encourage these comments as well. If you have several people at the table, make sure everyone has the opportunity to speak. Some children (and parents) are quite talkative, while others are not so much. Therefore, it is important to ask questions of each person and make sure everyone brings something to the evening's conversation. Consider ways to get your children to expand on what they are saying. "Tell me more" is always a good response, along with, "How did that make you feel?"

As young children mature to around six to ten years of age, continue to celebrate their ideas. Bringing up an idea or subject should be a pleasant experience for them. Their ideas may be immature or maybe even ridiculous from an adult perspective; nevertheless, hear them out. We had a rule in our house that put "stupid" in the category of bad words, such as "shit" or "damn." This rule was important because, in families with more than one child, it is often not the parent who shuts down the child's ideas, but the siblings who do so. "That's a stupid idea," may resonate for some of you. Whether you heard it from a parent, a sibling, or a friend, this phrase can discourage children's voice and cause them to filter their ideas based on what others will think.

To encourage young people to bring ideas and creative solutions to a conversation or problem, consider the following tactics. The first strategy is to make sure appreciation is part of your conversations. In her book, *Redirecting Children's Behavior*,[17] Kathryn Kvols recommends appreciation feasts where each person shares something they appreciate about the other family members. It can be as simple as, "I am thankful Ian helped me with the dishes last night," or "I appreciate how Brittany wakes up with a smile every morning." Even if the whole family isn't willing to play along, parents should take time every day to tell each child something they appreciate about them. Keep it simple; keep it light. "I like how your shirt looks good with those pants," or, "It looks like you and your friend really enjoy each other's company." When we remind children of their positive traits and actions, they become more comfortable in their own skin and are more likely to share their ideas.

Questioning

A second strategy to encourage children to voice their opinions is to prompt them with questions. Similar to the "tell me more" strategy used with very young children, this age group might respond to more thoughtful prompts. Have them tell you about their dreams. Listen intently by making eye contact, nodding your head, smiling, and interjecting with supporting sounds or words. For young people who are quiet and thoughtful, several shorter conversations work, just as well as long ones. Watch for times when they are ready to talk and encourage them. One of my daughters is not a morning person. Trying to talk to her in the morning is frustrating for everyone. However, once the sun goes down, she is animated and talkative. Work with your child's natural cycles. Other questions for this age group include questions focused on imagination and surreal ideas. What if horses could fly? If you could be any animal, what would it be? If you could change the color of the sky, what color would you make it? How many suns would you put up there? A strong imagination is equally as important as a strong intellect.

Reading and Writing

Finally, a third strategy is to use reading and writing as a means for children to feel heard. Continue to read with your children, even when they are old enough to read on their own. Read a book aloud to the whole family and talk about it together. Ask your child questions about the characters, how they are similar to each of you and how they are different. Share likes and dislikes, and remember to honor differences. Alternatively, get two copies of a book and read on your own; come back to discuss it after you've both read it. Books are great conversation starters, but so are other mediums. Share movies, video games, and sports with your child; follow their interests. I used journaling with one of my older daughters. When she was young, we explored a joint journal. I would write a page about something and then ask her a related question. She would take the journal and write back to me. It was a great way to find their voice for a child who was more comfortable processing ideas before sharing. We can engage with our children in many ways to give them opportunities to have a voice and learn about their own imaginations and opinions. Enjoy the process!

MY CHILD WON'T STOP TALKING

Over my years of work, some parents have come to me with the opposite problem—a child who won't stop talking. First, count yourself lucky. Then, look for ways to direct the energy of the conversation. Support your child in learning to stay on topic, organizing their thoughts, and making sure everyone has the opportunity to talk. A strategy used in a variety of environments is the idea of a talking stick. It doesn't have to be a stick; anything will work (ball, spoon, pen). Whoever holds the talking stick is the person who can talk. When they are done, they pass it to someone else in the room and it becomes that person's turn. Classrooms with young children use this strategy all the time, so children can learn not to talk over each other or interrupt. Healthy, satisfying conversation is something we all learn how to do. Support your child by providing ample opportunities to practice, learn, and become competent.

Teenagers

For teenagers, having a voice in conversations takes a new direction. As children enter their teen years, they begin to notice the world around them. They start to see injustice, and they want to address inequities. Studies at school become more intellectual, and teenagers have more exposure to current events, issues, and new ideas through school and through the media.

I opened this section on children's voices with a story about my teenage nephew. These conversations can be awkward in the beginning. It may be the first time your teenager has felt such a level of passion or commitment. The words come out with a fierceness that is new to them. Let them explore these conversations. Recognize, once again, your teenager is in another learning phase. The awkwardness will transform into articulated arguments, but they need practice to master the art of conversation. Pointing out areas to improve is far less effective than modeling respectful conversation. Engage in these conversations fully. Share your perspective and bring in counter perspectives to ensure your teenager thinks about both sides of the argument. Your teenager is beginning to see how an individual can make a difference, what it feels like to have an opinion, and how to express their perception of what is right and wrong with the world. It is an exciting time for them.

In my family, both immediate and extended, topics about food-related controversies often emerge at our dinner table. These topics include hunting for food, GMO production of vegetables, the treatment of livestock, families who experience food insecurity, and the resurgence of the victory garden, to name a few. Not everyone agrees on all of these issues, but our family creates a safe space for everyone to share their views. We make sure everyone gets a chance to talk, share informational resources, and respect the different opinions around the table. When each of us has a voice, from the very youngest to the oldest, our lives are richer; we provide our children with the opportunity to learn new skills in the safety and security of our homes, so they can go out into the world and make a difference.

EXPERTISE TO SHARE

At this point in the chapter, I have covered two ways to empower everyone in our homes—ensure children are provided ample opportunities to make choices and encourage them to have their own voice. This final section focuses on teaching and sharing expertise, not parents teaching children, but the other side of the coin. An excellent tool for empowering others is to learn from them, to let them share their expertise, and to support them in feeling they have something to give. When our children are able to teach us or others, they begin to find their own strengths and interests.

Show Me

Ask very young children to show you what they have learned. As they begin to grasp foundational concepts such as colors, numbers, and letters, have them demonstrate what they are learning. "Show me" is a phrase you can use to encourage children to show off what they have learned and how far they have come. It is also an excellent way to reinforce the lesson. When a child explains a new concept to an adult, the concept becomes even more integrated into their knowledge base. At this age, children are full of enthusiasm for learning. They learn through play, imagination, and from their schoolmates and teachers. Tap into this enthusiasm and have them show you at least one thing they learned each day. When they tell you what the letter "A" sounds like, share in their discovery.

Passions

When children reach the later years of elementary and middle school, they are in a position to share new knowledge with those around them. As they explore sports, artistic activities, or involvement with nature and animals, their experience expands beyond schoolwork. Ask them to share their passions with you. If they are learning to play an instrument, have them teach you to play a chord on the guitar or a scale on the piano. If they are a member of 4-H, scouts, or other youth organizations, you can have them show or explain to you how to saddle a horse, shoot a bow and arrow, or start a campfire. Our children represent a youthful, enthusiastic energy in our lives and it benefits everyone involved to recognize how we learn from each other, regardless of age.

Explain

Just as our young children benefit from the "show me" phrase, our older children can benefit from "explain to me." The process of teaching, demonstrating a new skill, or explaining a new concept supports individuals in several ways. Teaching enhances the neurological connections in the brain, builds confidence in the emotional self, strengthens relationships, and develops resilience. Creating an environment in which a child can share their expertise creates an environment where you won't need punishment. A child doesn't need to resort to misbehavior for attention, or act out because they feel disempowered. Instead, they are able to express their true nature as a contributing member of the family by sharing information and expertise. In addition to sharing expertise with you, encourage children to help each other. Not only does the child who is learning benefit, but so does the one teaching. Siblings, cousins, and neighbors can all work together to teach and empower children in the family as well as the neighborhood.

Engage

Your teenager has much to share with you, and parents who are open to learning from them have much to gain. This is the time when true connection between parents and children can begin to blossom. Witnessing my youngest daughters become teenagers who were engaged with their parents, family, friends, and teachers was the most gratifying part of my "grand experiment." Because they grew up without the pressure of parents pushing against their spirits, they didn't need to push back during their adolescence. I have warm memories of them joining conversations with family friends who found them to be mature, kind, and engaging. The number of disagreements was minimal, and the disagreements were readily resolved. Even though they may have had different interests and strengths, they created strong bonds and are the best of friends. A punishment-free environment meant they weren't competing for attention or blaming each other in order to stay out of trouble. In contrast, though, if an individual spends their childhood with parents who push them to behave a certain way, living under the threat of punishment if they don't comply, they will most likely push back when they reach adolescence and finally feel they have the ability to do so.

If you have worked to maintain a healthy relationship and have eliminated punishment as a means to control behavior, your adolescent will be engaged with life, will be hungry to learn, and will be mature enough to tackle adult problems. This is a time to let their light shine and have them not only share their expertise with you, but also begin to share it with the world. They may choose to go out into the workforce and experiment with steady work. They may choose to dive into a volunteer project and share their passion by cleaning trails or assisting the elderly. They may start their own company. The world is full of stories of young people who share themselves and their expertise early in life. As a parent, your role is simply to cheer them on, provide the necessary safety net should they fail (always the best way to learn), and love them.

~~~~~~~~~~~~~~~~~~~~~~

"Once a child reaches sixteen to eighteen years old, your influence will be mostly complete, and research suggests their peers will become their source for guidance."

~~~~~~~~~~~~~~~~~~~~~~

If your child is already a teenager when you picked up this book, it is not too late. Begin to have conversations with them about punishment. You can start a punishment-free approach to parenting at any time in your child's upbringing. You will see an amazing transformation with the first conversation. Sharing your intent to trust your teenager and eliminate punishment will bring great relief, and you will see them blossom. Encourage your teenager to share their passions by asking about what they care about. Ask them to share their favorite subject in school. Ask them what they appreciate about their best friend. Through asking questions, your teenager will begin to realize their input is important, and you care about what they think. You will be acknowledging their worth and their individuality, and you will be letting them know they have expertise to share. Once a child reaches sixteen to eighteen years old, your influence will be mostly complete, and research suggests their peers will become their source for guidance.[18] Your role is to provide support as they experiment with adulthood, hopefully from the safety of your home. Your role is not to tell them what to do; this approach only increases their need to push back. Remind them of their strengths, that they are experts in their own life, and they have the knowledge and experience to do what's right for them. Regardless of their age, our children feel empowered when we acknowledge their strengths.

It is important to keep power in mind when parenting from a punishment-free approach. Continue to ask who naturally holds the power in a family. Who has to earn power? Who feels powerless? Power imbalance is the foundation for much of the strife in our families. To address the imbalance of power, families can ensure everyone has the opportunity to make choices, feel heard, and share their passions. I have shown why these strategies are important to the developmental process of our children, and I have outlined the importance of recognizing how our families provide a safety net for children to grow into healthy and confident adults. It is hard to watch a child make a wrong decision or stumble through a conversation while trying to state their opinion, but preventing them from making choices or sharing their ideas only makes children feel disempowered and dependent. This approach will eventually lead to frustrated children and resentful parents. Children have a natural eagerness within them and they will thrive when they can express it. Using the tactics described here, your will child feel in control and have a sense of agency, which will minimize misbehavior. The result will be a homelife where the need for punishment won't even come up because everyone will feel empowered. As noted in "The Enlightened Princess" story, take time to look deeply within each of your children. See the wonder and value of each one. Use your time together to acknowledge them, treat them as equals, and share the wealth of power.

As we wrap up the foundational information on punishment and power, it's time to consider how you can put this information to use. What does punishment-free parenting look like for you? How do you engage with your children and guide them when behavior needs correcting? The next chapter covers common parenting hazards that trip us up every day, and we will then dive into "Part II: Your Parenting Journey," a series of chapters organized by age to help you answer these questions for each developmental stage of your child.

CHAPTER 4

TOP 5 PARENTING HAZARDS

NOW THAT WE HAVE SOME BACKGROUND into *why* we want to incorporate punishment-free strategies as parents, let's look at *how* we do this work. When I was considering how I would raise my two young daughters without punishment, several parenting challenges loomed on my horizon. Having already been on a typical journey with my two older children, I knew I would soon have to address challenges such as mornings and bedtimes. What I discovered though, as I stayed steadfast in my commitment to punishment-free parenting, was that I could address even these tough areas if I focused on treating my children with kindness and incorporating creative solutions. Like most parents, I had a lot of questions. If we were to take punishment out of our parenting tool belt, how do we engage with our children when their behavior is disruptive? How would we support appropriate behavior? How would we help them learn to differentiate between right and wrong?

In this chapter, I provide a variety of alternative options for supporting the healthy growth of children through what I call the Top 5 Parenting Hazards. On your parenting journey, as with any journey, you will inadvertently run into pot holes, construction zones, and speed bumps. These hazards are the common situations when parents and children feel frustration and even desperation. These challenges sometimes sneak up on you when you least expect it. If you learn how to relate effectively to your children during these more trying times, it will make a big difference in your overall relationship and will support your journey in punishment-free parenting. The Top 5 Parenting Hazards include sleeping, bedtime, mornings, shopping, and eating. The options I share here to help you navigate these challenges are not prescriptions. Consider this chapter to be a goody bag full of ideas you can try. They may or may not work in your particular situation, but they will hopefully inspire you. Open your eyes and heart to possibilities. You are not your mother or father, and you are not your grandmother or grandfather. You are unique and so are your children. Each situation, each relationship, each day, and maybe even each hour will call on you to creatively address the needs of your child (and yourself) as you support their growth without punishment. Let's start with sleeping.

~~~~~~~~~~

"The importance of consistency came up in all of the research. If you decide to co-sleep, co-sleep most nights. If you decide to have your child sleep separately, make it your ritual."

~~~~~~~~~~

1. SLEEPING

The topic of sleeping, one of our most basic needs, can be quite controversial, especially for infants and young children. This is a good time to remind you that this book is not about right and wrong; it is about inviting parents to think critically and understand there are many ways to support their children. This is simply information, not a rulebook. Having a baby is usually synonymous with sleep deprivation. Well-intentioned friends and family members try to prepare new parents for the looming challenge of caring for an infant 24 hours a day, 7 days a week. Correct answers and panaceas really don't exist for the first few weeks of having a baby. When I had my first baby, my obstetrician actually said, "Just get through the first six weeks. Then it will get better." I thought it was strange advice, but in hindsight realized it was probably what I needed to hear. On the other hand, the first weeks with your baby can also be the most magical. You are getting to know and fall in love with a brand-new person. Sleep deprivation is a small price to pay.

In these early days, one of the first questions parents consider is where to have the baby sleep. Different cultures, times, and personal needs all factor in to a new family's sleeping arrangement. If you do your research, you will find qualified experts supporting all of your options. Clinicians will tout the importance of never taking your baby to bed with you due to safety issues. Academic researchers will encourage co-sleeping, citing research that suggests it supports a healthier baby and mom.[19] Whether or not you decide to have your baby sleep with you in your bed, in the same room in a separate bed, or in a separate room, the decision is yours.

The importance of consistency came up in all of the research. If you decide to co-sleep, co-sleep most nights. If you decide to have your child sleep separately, make it your ritual. With four children spanning several years, I experienced both options. My first two children started out sleeping in a bassinette next to the bed and later transitioned to a crib in a separate room. For my second two children, we instituted co-sleeping. I felt most comfortable sleeping in the middle of the bed with the baby on the side. My husband installed a bumper on the baby's side, so she couldn't fall out. They stayed with us until they were young toddlers and could move into a toddler bed. All of our children were always welcome in our bed if they needed some nighttime comfort. I would hear little footsteps approach when one of them had a nightmare or if a scary storm roused them from their sleep. The question of intimacy often comes up for families considering co-sleeping, but after talking with couples, I've found they can be creative in finding time to be together. A soundly-sleeping infant won't wake with quiet intimacy and as one couple stated with a smile, "There are other rooms in the house to explore."

I watched the benefits found in the co-sleeping research play out with my children. The primary benefit for the child is a strong sense of security and attachment to the mother while they are young (though it does not seem to carry over once children are older). Co-sleeping supports better sleep for baby, but it does not for all moms. Although some moms get better sleep when sleeping separately, it has its own set of challenges. The outdated strategy of letting a child "cry it out" can be extremely stressful and contributes to poorer sleep for everyone. To avoid hours of crying, a parent must make several trips to the crib for consolation while the baby learns to sleep alone.

Research shows attachment and security are the attributes most affected by your choice of sleeping arrangement. Most children who initially share a bed with their parents have a stronger sense of attachment, whereas children who sleep in a separate bed typically rely on additional sources of security. I have memories of my first child's need for security devices. She had a beloved stuffed puppy she couldn't live without, and we once had to drive back to a hotel (thirty minutes both ways) to retrieve it because she was inconsolable. She also was more dependent on a pacifier. I have no recollection of security items (blankets, stuffed animals, etc.) for my second two children. Of course, every child is unique. What works for one child may not work for a second or a third. Some children may be too active at night which could make co-sleeping a challenge. Others may thrive on physical closeness and relish being near mom during the night. Remember, you are getting to know this brand-new person; so listen and observe intently.

2. BEDTIME

Bedtime rituals also vary by child. Bedtime is a time of separation for children. Some are secure and know they will wake to find a parent there each morning, others are fearful and hesitate to leave their parent's side, and others are so full of life and joy, they don't want the pleasure of the day to end. For parents, however, bedtime is a chance to unwind and take a break from the daily tasks of parenting. Some parents take time after putting their children to bed to catch up on work, connect with their partner, or catch up with friends. Children can sense your desire for this break, and if you rush bedtime, children will push back (remember the hand pushing exercise) and attempt to drag it out in order to remain the center of your attention. Our goal in eliminating punishment from your relationship with your child is to avoid situations where punishment feels like the only option.

This conversation regarding bedtime reminds me of an exercise I did with parents through the *Redirecting Children's Behavior* work.[20] It is an easy one to do at home with your partner or with a friend. In the near future, take a few minutes to go through the "Attention Exercise."

ATTENTION EXERCISE

1. Select one parent to role-play the parent and the other to role-play the child.

2. The child has just found a beautiful stone and is excited about the stone and wants to share the wonder of it.

3. In the first part of the exercise, the parent acts distracted, busy preparing a meal or finishing a project. The child brings the stone to the parent and desperately tries to show them. The child pulls on their clothes, talks incessantly, and does anything and everything they can to get the parent's attention.

4. After completing this part of the exercise, role play the same scenario, this time having the person playing the parent stops whatever they are doing to give the child their undivided attention, oohing and aahing over the stone, acknowledging the child.

5. Have the child share how they felt in each situation.

Adapted from *Redirecting Children's Behavior* by Kathryn Kvols

The adult roleplaying the child usually shares very different feelings in each scenario. When ignored, they feel as if they must continue until they can show off their beautiful stone, even if takes an hour. In the second scenario, the person roleplaying the child is ready to go off and continue with their day within a matter of minutes.

This exercise represents an important component of your bedtime ritual with your child. If it feels rushed, like something to quickly get through, your child will feel the need to connect and resist all efforts to bring an end to it. Their desire for your undivided attention will have staying power beyond what you can imagine. Alternatively, remind yourself this time is an opportunity to connect and support your child in transitioning from an active day to peaceful rest. Numerous bedtime rituals exist around the globe. Many parents incorporate warm baths, storytelling or reading, snacks, teddy bears, and stuffed puppies, to name a few. Find the ritual that works best for your child, follow it consistently, be present, and most importantly, make sure it doesn't feel rushed. You will find it takes less time (like the stone exercise) if you devote yourself to the process.

3. MORNINGS

Ah, mornings. Especially true for working parents, mornings bring their own collection of challenges and joys. I've consistently mentioned how each child is unique, as is each parent. Some of us are morning larks, and others are night owls. Some of us sleep well, and others are grateful for even one good night of sleep within a week. All these factors, plus the other quirky characteristics we hold, add up to challenging mornings. I have many morning stories, such as the morning I threatened to leave my daughter at home alone if she didn't get herself dressed (don't do that). There were many mornings I ran into Walmart to get slippers for pajama day or a last-minute bottle of glue for a class assignment. (A note to new parents—if you end up at Walmart to buy slippers, bring scissors to cut the elastic band between them so your child can actually wear them). The primary challenge with mornings, however, is we have so much to do in such a short amount of time. We want to get as much sleep as possible, but we also want to get to work or school on time. As with bedtimes, when we try to rush children, they typically respond with resistance because they are human. Two secrets I have uncovered about mornings are give yourself plenty of time and don't expect perfection.

Time is important for you and your child. Some children need a lot of time, and others may not need as much. In my family, we have a child with a slow, even temperament, which means they really don't have it within them to hurry. This temperament has many advantages, but it works against getting out the door on time. These children need extra time to slowly transition into their day, ponder, wake up, and ensure they don't have to run down the stairs or hurriedly brush their teeth. Expecting them to get ready as quickly as you do will only lead to frustration. Schedule their wake-up time to give them the mornings they need. In considering the pros and cons of a peaceful temperament, sometimes mislabeled a lazy temperament, I frequently reference a study I read many years ago, so I am unable to provide the reference. The book was about nature versus nurture and dealt with the question of whether children are born with specific traits or if they develop certain traits based on their environment. A study on twins separated at birth and later reunited as adults found one set of twins who both had an overwhelming desire for cinnamon. What was most interesting to me was how each set of parents described their child. One set stated, "Our child is a terrible, picky eater. All she ever wants is cinnamon." The second set described, "My child is a great eater. She will eat anything as long as we put cinnamon on it." They both had the same trait but parents with different perspectives. A child who didn't get the hurry gene is an amazingly calm and patient individual. Is your child lazy or simply even tempered?

So how do you ensure everyone has the time they need? Begin with the end in mind. If 7:30 a.m. is the deadline for everyone to be in the car with lunches, books, and school projects ready to go, then back track from there. How much time does breakfast take? How much time does your child with a calmer temperament need to simply get out of bed, let alone get themselves dressed? Build in enough time, so you don't have to rush your children. Will mornings still occur when everyone is scrambling because you couldn't find your left shoe or keys? Of course. However, minimizing the rush of mornings can go a long way in supporting a family environment where you don't need to coerce children to comply with threats of punishments.

"...reaching for perfection in the morning only creates more stress for everyone during an already stressful time."

The second component to supporting mornings is to not expect perfection. In fact, don't even expect good. You are shooting for decent. When children are infants, something you may take for granted is your ability to dress your baby. You pick out the clothes and make sure they fit and look cute and adorable. When your child becomes old enough to have their own say in the matter of clothes, this pleasure goes out the window. You need to let decent be your bar at that age. In the grand scheme of life, does it really matter if your child's pants and shirt don't match for preschool? The answer is no. Your child's newfound ability to select their own clothes, dress on their own, and feel good about the process is much more important than an inappropriate color combination. Let it be okay if a child's hair is a little messy, or accept breakfast will be a granola bar every once in a while, instead of a healthy meal. The bottom line is reaching for perfection in the morning only creates more stress for everyone during an already stressful time. Save those battles for cousin Carl's wedding. Events come up when clothes should match and hair should be combed, and these are important lessons to learn too. A note of caution, though. As children mature, they sometimes need support in knowing how to dress appropriately and the importance of hygiene. To send a ten-year-old to school, knowing they will be embarrassed for what they are wearing in order to "teach them a lesson" is a form of punishment. Don't do it.

4. SHOPPING

Standing in line for the cashier recently, I observed a mom with two young daughters. The girls were squirmy, impatient, and easily distracted by the merchandise lined up for customers to peruse while waiting. It reminded me of shopping with my children and the additional energy it required. When we are at home with our children, our guard is down. We have created a safe space, we have no concern that things may get broken—they belong to us—and we use a relaxed and comfortable communication style. When we transition to the outside world, especially retail stores, we are in for a different experience. Our children are in a strange space. If something gets broken, we are responsible, we want to avoid judgement from fellow shoppers, and we have to be prepared for what feels like the never-ending cycle of "I want" or "can we get" from children mesmerized by all of the shiny objects.

So how do we create a normalized experience for parents and children and find strategies to use in place of threats and punishments? Again, the best way to eliminate punishment as a tool in your parenting toolbelt is to minimize the times when we feel pushed toward the use of punishment to control behavior. The best solution I have uncovered is to balance your needs with the wants of your children. When children are very young, the balance is between your need for safety and their desire to explore. One method I used was the "one finger touch." Children are naturally curious and want to pick up everything to look at it. This instinctual drive is a positive attribute; it's how we learn. We can threaten, reward, and punish all we want; we won't dampen this important characteristic. To appease this instinct, I would allow my young children to touch new items with a single finger. It gave them satisfaction and resolved their curiosity, and it reassured me they wouldn't pick up the expensive item and break it. Additionally, we would always hold hands to ensure their personal safety, and, as they got a little older, we made sure one hand was on the grocery cart or stroller.

ONE FINGER TOUCH

Instead of saying "Don't touch," over and over again, the one finger touch is an alternative you can use in most stores.

1. When you enter the store, remind your child to use the one finger touch while in stores.
2. When your child reaches for something that catches their eye, demonstrate how they can explore it by using one of your fingers to gently touch the object.
3. Ask your child if they want to try and encourage them to touch the object with just the tip of their finger.

This strategy satisfies their insatiable curiosity and gets you both through your shopping experience without tears, tantrums, or yelling.

As children grow older the challenges at the store shift from supporting their intense curiosity to attending to their newly emerging desire for material objects. They see clothes, sporting equipment, candy, favorite foods, games, etc., and they long to own them. This is not a natural desire like our innate curiosity, but it is a desire fed by our culture—by commercials, media, and conversations with friends and family. The desire to own and have material goods is integral to the capitalistic society of Western culture. As a parent, you will have to address this longing each time your children join you for a shopping outing. Sometimes, you won't even have to go out since the lure of shopping and buying is now available on phones and computers.

Several strategies are available to support your child in learning about money, ownership, longing, and saving. Each family is unique, each circumstance varies, and, of course, each child is different. As you might expect, there are no right and wrong answers or specific ways to approach the situation. Getting to know your child and their unique approach to life is foundational in building a positive relationship without the need for threats or punishment. To begin, support your child in understanding the notion of value and money. Even at a relatively young age, you can share with children where your money comes from, such as "Mommy and Daddy go to work every day, and because we give our time to the company, they give us money in exchange. We can then use the money to buy the things our family needs. Some of the money pays for our house, some pays for our cars, some for our food and for our clothes, and some of it pays for gifts." Help your child understand the concept of money and how people earn it and use it. Before you leave the house to go to a store, have a conversation about how much money you plan to spend and what items you plan to purchase. Modeling the idea of a budget will translate into a young adult who sees money as a tool, rather than an emotional crutch. The second strategy to use before leaving the house is to see if your child believes they need something specific while you are out. Having the conversation at home, without the influence of shiny objects, will go a long way in avoiding the constant "Can I get the teddy bear, *please*?" The important component of this strategy is to agree to some items on a regular basis. Have a conversation about how much candy is healthy. Is it one piece of candy each week at the grocery store? Is it a special treat once a month? Provide opportunities for your children to plan to buy items and then buy them for them. A life of lack only creates stronger desire. Having a balance of patience and receiving will create balanced emotions within your child when it comes to material goods.

"Your goal is to engrain in your child positive feelings about money by showing them a variety of ways to engage with it to bring joy to themselves and others."

The next level in learning about money and shopping is to support your child in having money of their own. In some families, an allowance is allotted to each child, so they can experience managing money. In other families, children earn money through chores. A child may contribute to the household by unloading the dishwasher or taking care of family pets. Parents then allot a reasonable amount of money for their work, mimicking what happens in adulthood with jobs and careers. A word of warning is do not let this situation turn into a power struggle. If your children are doing activities to earn money, the onus is on them to complete the work. If they choose not to do the work, they won't earn the associated money—no emotion, and no struggle. Finally, some families support children with looking for ways to earn money outside of the home. They can rake leaves for a neighbor, walk their grandma's dog, or set up a lemonade stand out front. Listen to your child, observe them at play, have a lot of conversations, and their individual strengths will emerge. As children acknowledge these strengths, they can then determine what kind of contribution they can make.

Once your child has access to money, whether through an allowance, gift, or job, you support them by providing resources on how to use money. Work with them to figure out how to save for a larger purchase. Model for them how donating money to a cause or person they care about feels good and keeps the cycle of kindness flowing. Your goal is to engrain in your child positive feelings about money by showing them a variety of ways to engage with it to bring joy to themselves and others.

5. EATING

How, when, and what we eat is one human characteristic with a wide range of variability. Consider your own eating habits. Think about how you ate as a child, as a young adult, and now as a more mature adult. Not only are your eating habits different from the habits of people around you, but they have changed over time, perhaps due to available resources or health or body weight issues. The bottom line is eating habits vary widely. Each of your children also has a different approach to food with different likes and dislikes. In some families, eating is the source of a significant number of power struggles. Each culture has set times for eating each day, and many traditions exist around what kinds of foods are served when and by whom. Most social gatherings involve food, and it is often the greatest gift we can give to someone in need. No wonder food carries such a charge.

One method to ensure your family life has a supportive environment for eating is to avoid labeling your children with phrases such as, "He is a picky eater," or, "She hates vegetables," or, "She'll only eat cinnamon." When you label your child, especially with a negative label, you will be asking for a battle. From their perspective, how they eat is exactly what works for them. Forcing them to adapt to your way of eating or suggesting that something about how they eat is "less than" incites a need to prove you wrong. On the flip side, we also must acknowledge that children need guidance around food. I've often stated that if we didn't give children guidance around food, they would have pizza for dinner every night. (Though, if your child wanted pizza every night, you could simply ensure a variety of toppings was available and present their meals in the form of pizza, but I digress.)

To support your parenting experience around eating, it is important to remember a growing body and brain have different nutritional needs than adults. A child's body is in constant flux, moving, growing, resting, rejuvenating, and then starting the process all over again. The most consistent observation about a child's eating and activity levels is that they won't be consistent. It is not unusual for a three-year-old to eat very little on Monday, then more than a full-grown adult on Wednesday. You can drive yourself crazy trying to ensure your child eats well three times a day, every day. Their bodies simply do not function the same as ours. Their need for nutrients, rest, and physical activity varies considerably from day to day, sometimes even hour to hour. Even a teenage body will fluctuate dramatically. Not only are they continuing to grow, but their bodies are introducing surges of hormones into the mix.

The U.S. has come a long way in developing nutritional guidelines, and the latest trend is to support the idea of a total diet. Rather than focusing on specific foods and labeling them as good and bad, the recommendation is to consider the entirety of one's diet. If vegetables, fruits, water, and protein are available throughout your day, it is okay to include a sugary drink, dessert, or glass of wine. The same is true for your children. As long as the majority of what they eat is healthy, providing them with the opportunity to enjoy treats throughout the day is not only okay, but it is also healthy. The Academy of Nutrition of Dietetics supports this philosophy, stating how strictly avoiding sugary foods creates a sense of deprivation which increases desire.[21] If a specific food emerges as one your child's desires, and you never allow them to have it, it becomes a forbidden fruit. As soon as they can find a way to get it, they will more than likely eat more than if you had let them enjoy it in moderation. Additionally, the constant power struggle can pull you into a cycle of punishment and threats in order to put an end to the conflict.

In caring for the nutritional needs of your child, remember they have not been as conditioned as we are regarding food and still receive strong signals from their bodies regarding what they need. This is evident in the variability of how much a child eats. Some days they eat very little, and other days they eat so much you wonder where it all goes. These cycles are normal, and trying to force a child to eat more when they are not hungry, or withholding food when they are, begins to quiet these signals. You want them to listen to their bodies. This attunement will serve them well throughout their lives. So, what is your role in supporting healthy habits and encouraging the intake of healthy foods?

First, remember you are helping them to grow into an adult who knows both *how* to eat and *what* to eat. We have already talked a little bit about how to eat. Encourage your child to listen to their bodies. Talk to them about feeling hungry and support them in eating throughout the day. If an evening comes when everyone is sitting around the table, and your child claims they are not hungry, respect their choice. We have a strategy at our house we call the "one bite rule." Everyone has to take one bite of each item served for dinner. This tactic serves a couple purposes:

- If a child is simply tired or frustrated (and actually hungry), taking a bite will jumpstart their body to recognize their hunger.
- It exposes children to a variety of tastes without forcing them to eat something they didn't initially like.

The outdated practice of "cleaning your plate," or ensuring we aren't throwing away food that could support starving children, is harmful to healthy eating habits. When we force a child to eat, it not only disempowers them, but it also sets up poor eating habits.

Second, remember what we have learned so far regarding power, control, voice, and acceptance of how it is okay to make mistakes. Your child may be at a friend's house and end up eating too much sugar. They'll feel the negative consequences in their bodies, and you can have a conversation (not a lecture) about moderation and enjoying sweets every now and then. If you put too much emphasis on the rights and wrongs of eating, you will create tension around food, which will only lead to yet another visit to the therapist. All joking aside, let food be an enjoyable part of your relationship with your child. Explore it together. Cook together. Garden together. Grocery shop together. Overindulge every now and then together. Celebrate this important part of our lives.

A final tip is keep only smaller quantities of sugary sodas, high-sodium snacks, and candy in the house (or none at all). Then, let these items be a treat when you go out. We didn't buy soda for the house, but we did let our children order it at restaurants. Additionally, we didn't restrict their choices if we went to a party or family gathering. Vacations were another time we would splurge and have some of the foods that weren't part of our regular diet. Experts in nutrition recommend not attaching labels such as "good" or "bad" to any food. Even as I write this section, I have to stop and purposefully remind myself not to identify some of these items as unhealthy. All foods should be part of our diet. Our goal is to ensure our diet includes vegetables, fruits, fresh water, protein, fats, eggs, and dairy, all of the nutrient-rich foods to support growing bodies and brains.

This chapter highlights the often reported struggles of the parent-child relationship. At the core of many of these areas is the disconnect between the schedule adults are on and the fluid nature of a child's life. When a child is absorbed in play, they are deeply involved in life. Their focus is attentive, all of their senses are engaged, and they are living fully. A call to the dinner table or a demand to stop because it is bedtime jars them away from their focus. Your role is to help them ease from one activity to the next. Give them some idea a change is coming, rather than unexpectedly demanding they stop what they are doing to respond instantly. Some people may value obedience in children, but we rarely value obedience in the adult world. As an example, a favorite bumper sticker of mine says "Well-behaved women rarely make history." As adults, we value initiative, critical thinking, self-reliance, and self-direction. We enjoy engaging with colleagues who share their own ideas, participate in team meetings, step-up to lead a project, or initiate a change. If we want our children to embody these characteristics, we need to give them opportunities to explore them as children. We do this through the small ways we interact with them.

By giving them a voice—having conversations about bedtimes, curfews, ideas about what would help to make for an easier morning—you will not only create a more peaceful household, but you will also contribute to the formation of an amazing adult. When the relationship is mutually respectful, and when children feel their opinions are honored and their voices heard, they will no longer feel a need to act out or misbehave. You will no longer need punishment and threats to control behavior. Children will continue to make mistakes (remember the importance of mistakes in the learning process). Take the time to correct, not punish. You are their support in their ultimate transition—moving from infancy to adulthood.

You are ready for your journey now. You have prepared yourself with the knowledge of *why* we want to parent without punishment, and you have spent some looking at *how* to begin that process with ideas on navigating power within the family. Finally, you have explored some actual strategies for addressing the hidden hazards we come across on the road to our final destination—healthy, active, and passionate adults. The next section of this book provides an age-by-age handbook on punishment-free parenting. As with all of the information in this book, some of it may sit well with you, and some of it may not. The ideas and examples are not rules; rather, they are strategies for you to explore. I provide them in order to give you the resources you need to engage with your child every day to support them on their unique journey. Enjoy!

PART II:
YOUR PARENTING JOURNEY

NOW THAT YOU HAVE A FOUNDATION in punishment-free parenting, your journey begins. Throughout these chapters, I'll share my journey to give you specific examples of parenting strategies beyond what I covered in the last section. It is important to recognize that age-appropriate parenting is important. As my children changed and matured, I had to change and mature in how I related to them and supported their journey from toddlerhood to young adulthood. I discovered that each age group typically has specific areas which challenge us as parents. The good news is this range of challenges ensures parenting is never boring. Just when you think you are in a good place and have figured out one age group, your child matures and presents a whole new set of challenges.

In the following four chapters, you can learn and experiment with ideas as we move through each age range. As you step into this section, you have several options. If you are pregnant or cradling an infant, start at the beginning and read your way through all of the chapters. If you already have children, you may want to start with the chapter associated with their age. I would recommend you eventually read all of them. Even if you are a parent of a teenager, there may be information in earlier chapters to spark your creativity, and you never know when you may need to support another parent with a young child. These chapters provide specific information you can use to navigate the ever-changing landscape of parenting and will prepare you to fully begin your punishment-free journey.

CHAPTER 5:
TODDLERS, AGES 2–4

I HAVE DISCOVERED PARENTING IS A JOURNEY with a changing landscape at each new bend. How I engaged with my two-year-old was quite different than how I engaged with my sixteen-year-old. In trying to keep with a punishment-free approach, I realized how important it is to understand the developmental stages of children. As an example, an average child under the age of four cannot comprehend the concept of lying. If we punish a child for lying when they are three years old, the lesson will go unappreciated by the child, and the parent will have suffered through a fruitless process. Telling lies is a complex process, one a three-year-old brain is not mature enough to tackle. Similarly, if you tried to teach algebra to most ten-year-olds, they would not be able to understand the abstract notion of variables. However, in just a few years, their brain will develop enough to think more abstractly. Because of the ever-changing landscape of your child's development, your parenting strategies have to be pliable, flexible, and adaptable, so they develop alongside your children. Constantly adjusting your parenting style and tactics is not easy. It's not like mastering a favorite meatloaf recipe and being able to repeat it again and again on Friday nights. Parenting takes creativity and a willingness to always be learning, observing your children, and finding new solutions. Take a few minutes to read "Guidance for Parenting Toddlers," and keep these ideas in mind as you read the chapter. We'll explore how to manage temper tantrums, handle hostility, approach resistance, and encourage imagination. Now, let's dive in to how to support a toddler.

GUIDANCE FOR PARENTING TODDLERS

- Each person on this planet is unique.
- A person's intention is positive from their point of view.
- Everyone is doing the best they can in any moment given their resources and their abilities.
- No child purposely misbehaves.
- The emotions of children are more intense than the emotions of adults.
- Children do not have filters nor do they have as much control over their emotions and behaviors as adults.
- Children's brains won't completely mature until they are 25 years old.
- Children have a natural desire for peace and harmony.
- Everyone needs to feel loved and have someone to love.

We'll start by taking a look at some commonly occurring toddler disruptions. How do these situations look from a punishment-free perspective?

TOUCHING

Let's begin with two-year-old challenges. Prior to children entering this stage of development, no form of discipline is needed. The brain of an infant is not mature enough to understand consequences, nor do they really have much control over their behavior. A child's infancy is a time for you to simply love and care for them. Enjoy their innocence and the purity of their being. However, as children move into their second year of life, their sense of self begins to emerge. At this age, children are profoundly curious and are just beginning to make sense of their world. As adults, they won't have any memory of being two, so we are still working with a brain in formation. At this age, a child is only beginning to recognize that their actions have consequences. Some days, they are better able to make this connection and other days, not so much. This developmental stage may tempt a parent to start slapping their young child's hand. Your child reaches for forbidden food (cookies or candy), they touch something in a store, or they even put themselves in danger by reaching toward a strange dog on a walk, all of which are unwanted actions you want to stop.

Redirecting

Each of these examples provides an opportunity to explore new approaches. Imagine your child is reaching for something they shouldn't have. It doesn't pose any danger, but you know it is not in their best interest to pursue it. It could be the food I used in my example, trash at the playground, or an older sibling's gaming device. In these examples, the forbidden item is not dangerous, so it is an opportunity to educate. When your child reaches for the trash, call their name to get their attention, and make a face indicating "yucky." Research has shown, even at a very young age, children recognize facial expressions. It is much better to communicate with them visually. You can add words to support the message (and contribute to their ever-growing vocabulary), but they will learn the most from your visible response to the forbidden item. Because they feel curious and inquisitive, find something healthy for them to explore instead. When they reach for the cookie, swap it out for a food you want them to have—perhaps a cup of applesauce or a handful of an appropriate snack. At the playground, you can playfully swoop them up and carry them to the slide or simply move away from the trash to dig in the clean sand. The gaming device may be more challenging. A young child knows their job is to learn how to be in this world. They watch everyone around them, especially older siblings. Seeing an older brother or sister pay so much attention to a gaming device sends the message this is an important item to know more about. In this case, it can be beneficial to find a way to give your young child an opportunity to at least explore the device without damaging it. Perhaps you hold the device and let your child press the buttons, or you can demonstrate how to hook it up to the console by pointing out the connections. Find a safe way for your child to explore it. A forbidden item only creates more desire and leads to a never-ending battle. You will be surprised how quickly your young child loses interest as soon as their curiosity is satisfied.

"...your child has an internal drive to touch everything to learn about this strange planet that is their home."

Alternatives

Because touch is how children learn at this age, they want to touch everything, regardless of where they are. This includes stores with expensive items, your friend's newly decorated house, or perhaps grandparents' houses where it has been awhile since young children were at play. Regardless of where you are, remember your child has an internal drive to touch everything to learn about this strange planet that is their home. These are environments where you need to use some discernment. We know the more we say no, the more children will push back—as with all humans. Your job as a creative parent is to find ways for your child to safely touch items in a new environment. Of course, there will be items they can't touch. In these cases, distraction is going to be one of your best tools. Plan ahead for these environments by bringing favorite toys, snacks, or books for your child to look through. Find a way to engage your child's innate desires by bringing items for them to explore, so they will leave your great aunt's china alone.

Alternatively, you can find a way for your child to safely touch items. I talked about my "one finger touch" strategy in Chapter 4. This technique gives you the opportunity to tell your child what they can do—touch carefully—rather than telling them what they can't do. Another option is to invite them to "explore with their eyes."[22] Anytime you can support positive behavior rather than focusing on negative behavior, it is a parental win. Let your toddler know what they *can* do. A common exercise is to tell your partner to close their eyes and then say to them "Don't think about a pink frog," or any other crazy image. When we speak about anything, we bring it to our attention. Putting the word "don't" in front of it can't stop the mind from bringing up a picture. To go through a store or be a guest in someone's home and repeatedly say "don't touch" exacerbates the situation, when all of their focus is on touching! Depending on the situation, another way to support your toddler in satisfying their curiosity is to ask them to sit down. With movement taken out of the picture, the environment is safer. You can then let them hold the item of interest in their lap. You will have to use your best judgement, but this may be a viable option for many items.

Another option is to simply remove yourself and your child from the environment. You may find yourself in a store with expensive items, at a time when you are tired, and your child is hungry—a triple threat. It is okay to take a break and calmly bring your child outside to shift everyone's attention away from the situation. Always stay with your child so you model the solution, rather sending them outside alone as a punishment. You want your child to learn they are loved, even when they are cranky. Sometimes, when we are cranky, changing the setting or taking a break can be helpful.

Define Boundaries

In some circumstances, touching is dangerous, and we need to support our children in learning when it is important to be cautious. Examples that come to mind are a hot stove, an unknown dog, or a sharp knife. Our role is to educate our children about the inherent dangers around them without creating unnecessary fear. To begin, imagine a time when you were confronted with a fearful situation. Perhaps it was while driving or walking alone. Our bodies innately react to dangerous situations. Your adrenaline courses, your reactions quicken, and you become extra vigilant to your surroundings. The same is true for your toddler. Even at a very young age, they respond to danger. Therefore, a very real danger will trigger the flight response in them, and they will have no problems staying away. If the unknown dog growls or displays aggressive behavior, your child will quickly run to safety, and the lesson will be quickly learned.

What about the not-so-obvious dangers? A hot stove or iron appears harmless. Mom uses the sharp knife laying on the counter every day. It does not seem as though it's something to fear. Your goal as a parent is to share these dangers by demonstrating both the intended use of these items, along with the possibility for injury. If your child is very young, keeping them at a distance is the best strategy. Don't set your child up on the counter next to a hot stove and keep knives out of reach. As your toddler matures, you have an opportunity to educate, by modeling how to use tools with inherent risks. Let's take the case of a hot stove. Your child sees you and your partner regularly using the stove. Remember their mission at this age is to figure out how everything on this planet works, and if you use something frequently, it must be important. Their curiosity is fueled, and they will want to learn all about it. When a child shows interest, it is best to address it rather than minimize it. Take a few minutes to demonstrate how it works. While in the process of cooking, pick up your child, take a spoonful of the food, let it cool enough to be safe, and then communicate "hot." Let them touch it to feel the warmth (it should not be hot enough to burn them). Then the two of you should taste it—they need to see the benefit of the tool. Once they are accustomed to how the stove works, their interest will wane. As they mature, they will begin to understand the concept of what's hot and will know not to touch it. The key to dispelling these dangers is to first maintain a safe environment (wall outlet covers, cabinet security hooks, etc.) and then to safely educate your child when you see their curiosity aroused.

Dr. Maria Montessori takes this concept to an even more advanced understanding. Her system of educating children is rooted in "following the child."[23] She understood the power of harnessing a child's curiosity and supporting them to learn about what is most interesting to them. Children in Montessori classrooms typically work individually on a variety of projects, exploring topics and ideas they find interesting, rather than being told what to study and when. If these ideas pique your interest, I encourage you to read more about the Montessori philosophy.

~~~~~~~~

"The terrible twos only become terrible
when we work against their natural
longing to explore and learn."

~~~~~~~~

We characterize this age as the terrible twos and threes, but those names are not accurate in the eyes of a two-year-old or a three-year-old. They see a world ripe for adventure, and they are finally mobile enough to begin exploring. It is our responsibility to support them in the exploration. The terrible twos only become terrible when we work against their natural longing to explore and learn. For some of us who are fearful or want to quickly intercede when a touch is inappropriate, our instinct might be to slap the hand of a young child. Although it is quick and certainly effective in the short run, it is important to stop and consider what the child is learning in the long run. They are too young to really understand bad behavior, so all they will learn is hitting and slapping are acceptable actions. They will also feel the sting of the slap. This message is more challenging to process. They internalize, "Here is someone who I am totally dependent on, who is basically an extension of myself, and they have caused me pain for a reason I don't quite understand."

Research has shown that not only do children who are slapped and hit resort to violence when frustrated, but it also stymies children's desire to explore and inhibits their learning.[24] Hand slapping is also ineffectual in teaching children not to touch. Hoping a young child will stop touching items is like hoping they will stop walking or hoping their teeth will stop coming in. Find ways for your young children to touch as much as possible, and when touching isn't an option, find other ways to support learning and exploration.

TANTRUMS

At the end of many long days, I have wanted to lay on the floor, kick my feet, and cry, but I know it isn't the responsible reaction to a rough day. Co-workers, finances, relationships, and all other assorted stresses can sometimes bring us to our knees. Our children are no different, and when they reach the end of their rope, they don't have the same level of restraint as adults, so they throw a tantrum. It is a way to release tension and get some attention. My children would always pick the most inopportune moments to have a tantum—at the grocery store, at the park, etc.—it was almost always a public place, and I would feel embarrassed as my child made a scene. What I realize in hindsight is many of these judgmental witnesses were once or currently parenting and completely understood my position. Hopefully, they also kept their judgment in check. Supporting a child who is having a tantrum is no fun. As a parent, you feel as though you have no control and simply want the tantrum to stop. The situation may tempt you to yell, threaten the child, and physically try to suppress the tantrum. When you are calmly reading this book, you can see how these negative responses only fuel the fire. When you're there in the moment, however, it can feel like the only option.

Understanding what causes a tantrum can help us consider ways to better address the issue. Emotions run through our bodies for a variety of purposes. In extreme situations, our fear keeps us safe. At other times, gratitude and appreciation bring calmness and peacefulness to support us in living a joyful life. A myriad of emotions materializes in between—anger, frustration, playfulness, and guilt, to name a few. I like to describe our ability to manage these emotions as we mature as water running through a faucet. By our mid-twenties, most of us have a decent amount of control over our emotions. We can feel the rush of the emotion (like the water coming through the faucet), but we have the ability to control how much comes through. Depending on the situation, we may fully open the knob to let the emotion through. At other times, we may only let a little of the emotion seep out since we are in our supervisor's office and would like to still have a job the next day. At other times, we may tighten the knob all the way. As we grow and learn, we practice managing our emotions by exploring how much to express, when it is appropriate, and with whom we are safe. At two years old, our little children have no idea a knob even exists. Their emotions come at them full force, with little or no restraint. Therefore, when they get tired, frustrated, or angry, they often lay on the floor, kick their feet, and cry.

Parents have many options to select from when their child has a tantrum. If your child is prone to tantrums, you may have tried each and every one. To approach a tantrum from the perspective of the parent, consider the following factors. First, is your child in a situation where throwing a tantrum could result in harm to them or another? Second, are you at home or in another safe place, or are you in a strange environment where neither you nor your child feel comfortable? Third, where are your emotions? Are you tired, hungry, frustrated, or angry? All of these factors come into play when considering how to handle a tantrum. Let's take a look at how some of our tantrum solutions can play out.

Remove

If the potential for harm is present, the solution is straightforward. You need to remove your child from the situation. An example might be a time when you are crossing a street, and your child puts up resistance. You might be outside in severe weather, or you might be near hard objects capable of causing injury if they start flailing about. In these examples, your first step needs to be to remove them from the environment. Swoop them up in your arms, ensuring you do so with care and warmth, but not to demonstrate they are in the wrong. Take them to a place where they can have their tantrum out of harm's way. Perhaps it is a grassy area if the tantrum started in the street, or it could also be your vehicle or home. Once they are in a safe environment, you can begin to use other strategies.

Now you need to assess your situation. Are you in a location where you have time and feel safe? If you are in your home and have a sense of calmness, it is, of course, the best situation. From this vantage point, you can see the tantrum for what it is—an outburst of emotion because your young child cannot adjust the knobs of their emotional faucet. This is not a time to add to the negative emotions by scolding, threatening, or yelling. You need to counter the negative outburst with calmness. Your approach will either slow the tantrum or prolong it. To slow the tantrum, support your child in letting off some steam.

Refocus

It is okay to lay on the floor, kick your feet, and cry for a few minutes. However, it will eventually be time to bring the child back to awareness, away from the strong emotions. You can do this in several ways. One is with a gentle touch (as long as you are calm). Simply put your hand on your child's heart (front or back) and rub a little. This strategy brings their awareness back to their body and the present. You can also use soothing language. Phrases you might use would include, "Wow. It looks like you are very [angry, hurt, frustrated]. Let's find out why and see what we may be able to do." You could also say, "I'm going to let you cry for a few minutes longer to get some of that [anger, pain, frustration] out. Then let's see about taking some time to do something quiet together, such as reading a book or playing with your blocks." If you are calm, stay with your child and let them know you will be there to support them. Once they start to calm down, make sure to include physical affection (hug them, hold them, take their hand) and find an activity they enjoy. It is also helpful to address the tantrum-causing issue. If they are tired, find a way for them to rest; if they are hungry, get them a snack; if they are angry, support them in finding a new way to express their anger the next time. You can invite them to use their words or yell into a pillow. Anger is a natural emotion all children will feel. Help them find ways to safely express it.

Regroup

Often when our young children feel frustrated, angry, or distraught, we find ourselves in the same position. Perhaps everyone in the family has had a long day, or dinner was delayed, or little time was available to take breaks and recharge. When you and your child both feel like having a tantrum, being calm, patient, and creative can be a challenge. Many of us may recall the infamous line, "if you don't stop crying, I'll really give you something to cry about!" Hopefully, this sentence sounds ridiculous. You are the giver of love and support, so why would you purposely make your child cry? However, when we are frustrated, angry, hungry, and tired, we say things we wouldn't say in an otherwise calm environment.

When you find yourself caught up in a swirl of tears and frustration, a few strategies are available:

- Use humor
- Take a break
- Ask for help
- Distract your child
- Simply say yes

One strategy is to use humor as the antidote. I recognize that when you are at the end of your rope, it can be hard to muster any humor; however, remember, you are attempting to get out of a bad situation. Perhaps you can lay down next to your child and actually have a tantrum too (in a funny way). You could take on a funny voice and talk about a waterfall of tears destined to drown the ponies—anything to get you to smile and hopefully get your child's attention back into the present (remember they feel lost in a sea of emotion). Use a favorite stuffed animal or puppet to talk to your child. Have this prop be silly, funny, and loving. Humor can diffuse situations quickly, and you will both start to feel better.

A second strategy you can use is to take a break. Sometimes you simply need a few minutes to calm yourself. Putting a child into a time-out is a punishment, and it will only add to their frustration, and escalate the tantrum. This solution (taking a break) puts you in time-out. Not really, but it does give you a few minutes to collect yourself. Make sure your child is safe and remains within ear shot so you can hear any change (if they are frustrated and crying, it's usually easy to hear them). Go to a nearby room, close your eyes, and take several deep breaths. Breathing will help you to calm down and recenter. Bring your energy and breath into your heart in order to calm your emotions. You may also find using imagery—recalling positive interactions with your child or a favorite beach vacation—can shift your energy. It should only take a few minutes to regain your composure, and when you become calmer, you will have the resources needed to help your child.

"You will be surprised at how insightful and creative children and adolescents can be in solving problems."

A third means to a happy ending is to simply ask for help. As parents we often feel we need to be superheroes. I recognize there might not always be someone around to help, but in instances when someone is available, remember it is okay to ask for help. In fact, modeling this behavior shows your child to do the same. In a world of big problems, it takes collaboration and teamwork to make significant change, so take advantage of the team around you. If your spouse or partner is home, look to them for assistance. Let them know you are at the end of your patience and could use their support with this challenge. Have them step into the situation with calmness and a desire to bring everyone back to a more normal level of emotion. If you have older children at home, they could also assist you. It is not their role to parent younger children; however, they can certainly participate in supporting a healthy family environment. You could ask an older child to stay with a little brother or sister for a few minutes while you take a break, or ask them if they have ideas on how to calm your toddler. You will be surprised at how insightful and creative children and adolescents can be in solving problems.

A fourth strategy is distraction. Sometimes, absolutely nothing will seem to be working in your favor. You may be in a location where you're not comfortable, your child is having a breakdown, and you are feeling short on patience. Perhaps you're at a wedding and have been active all day. Your child missed their nap, ate too much sugar, and you are tired. You ask your little one to sit still during the toast, and it becomes one too many requests for a tired toddler. They throw themselves on the floor, crying and screaming "no." It's your sister's anniversary celebration, and you don't want to leave, so what are your options? You need to stay calm. Even though you are tired and feeling short on patience, this is a time to call on your inner reserves. Remember, when you are calm, your thought process will be clearer and your creativity will be enhanced. Your best option at this juncture is to use a distraction. Telling your child to stop, hoping they will find it within themselves to calm down is futile. You need to shift their attention away from the current flood of emotion. Perhaps it is a paper napkin and pen for drawing, or perhaps it is a snack you have available. Perhaps it is something as simple as a funny face. Once the toast is over, lovingly pick up your child and find a place for both of you to take a break.

Finally, minimize the number of no answers your child hears. Balance the no answers with lots of yes answers to minimize the power struggles. Your child wants to explore, learn, grow, and have autonomy even at two and three years of age. Providing a safe way to explore and control their environment is critical. This approach will go a long way as they emerge into young children and adolescents.

Tantrums are one of the defining characteristics of the terrible twos and threes. Your best defense is a good offense. Remember your child needs more sleep than you do, remember their eating cycles can vary from day to day, and always remember their outbursts are not a reflection of you, your parenting, or their desire to wreak revenge. When you keep these factors in mind, you can find ways to prevent tantrums from happening in the first place. You can't always control your schedule, but on the many days you can, make sure you build in time for naps and quiet play. Keeping your child rested goes a long way in preventing breakdowns. You will also want to ensure they have access to healthy food throughout the day. Hunger and too much sugar are invitations for those strong emotions.

HOSTILITY

Once, when my two younger daughters were little, one of them hit the other in frustration over a game. My husband looked at me and asked, "Who taught her to hit?" I laughed and said, "No one taught her to hit. It is our job to teach her *not* to hit!" Young children act instinctively, and we all have the instinct to protect ourselves. When an object comes at us, we close our eyes to shield them. When a finger touches a hot surface, we instantly retract our hand. Similarly, when a child is angry, their first instinct is to strike out. Helping our children learn how to handle anger and frustration and teaching them how to manage those emotional faucet knobs is an important part of our work as parents. This is most certainly not the place to use punishment, especially physical punishment. I have shared the humorous image of a parent spanking a child repeatedly and with each spank, shouting: "Stop. Hitting. Your. Brother!" We can't tell our child not to do something and continue to do it ourselves.

We have many strategies at our disposal to teach children to use their words and other tools, rather than resort to physical violence when they are angry or frustrated. A great variety exists for children when it comes to anger management. Think of a continuum on which one end represents children who have milder personalities, and the other end represents children who are highly energetic and physical; you can imagine a wide range of personalities existing between these two extremes. Each of these personalities may need a unique approach to help them to learn not to hit. Consider a shy child who can find joy in almost any activity. When another child at the playground snatches a toy from them, they are often perfectly happy to find another object to play with. In contrast, some children are quite boisterous and physical. If a child snatches a toy from them, they will fight with intensity to get it back. What's even more interesting, is these two children can live in the same household—siblings from the same parents. Every child has their own personality, strengths, challenges, and temperament. This diversity is another reason creativity is so important to supportive parenting. Let's look at some forms of hostility.

Frustration

Your quiet and level-headed child may not need much support learning to handle anger and hostility. Their challenges will likely be elsewhere. They are most likely going to run into frustration over not being able to achieve a goal or communicate their needs. For example, they may be learning to maneuver a piece of playground equipment and after several unsuccessful attempts, find themselves frustrated and crying. For these children, simply support them with love and kindness. Telling them it will be okay will only frustrate them further. Assure them you will come back another day, so they know more opportunities will be available to master the skill. Should your child get angry and want to lash out, your best approach to help them learn is to gently hold their hands, and shake your head. They will not be in a place to understand language, but these physical gestures will help them understand that lashing out at others when they're angry or frustrated is not appropriate.

~~~~~~~~~~~~~~~~~~~~~~~~~~~~

"With an active child, helping them find safe ways to unleash their anger is a top priority."

~~~~~~~~~~~~~~~~~~~~~~~~~~~~

Anger

On the other end of the spectrum is the highly active child. Full of energy, they are a joy to be around when they are playing and engaged in positive activities. They will make you laugh and easily bring a smile to your face. However, when they are angry or frustrated their intensity will become more challenging. Just as they are the first to explore a new environment with zeal, they may also be first to get angry and physical with a playmate. As in our discussion on tantrums, an active child may not have very much control over their emotions or actions. Their initial response to an unfair situation (someone taking a toy, being told no by an adult, etc.) could be explosive. Your first goal is to minimize any harm to the other child, your child, and yourself. When an active child lashes out, it is with the same gusto they bring to all of life, and they will need support to manage it.

With an active child, helping them find safe ways to unleash their anger is a top priority. You need to do this work when your child is calm and focused. Once you recognize that your child needs support learning to handle strong emotions, you can begin to teach them when they are not angry. Although it seems like an overused example, hitting a pillow is an excellent way to release steam. When your child is somewhat calm, have a pillow fight where you lovingly knock each other around. They will begin to see the pillows as a tool, something they can toss around. The next time they are angry at a sibling and ready to physically attack, remind them people are not for hitting, and find a pillow they can hit or throw to release the anger. A young child will not be able to retain these lessons without repetition. It will take some patience on your part, but consistent instructions on what to do, rather than what not to do, will go a long way.

Strong Will

In addition to our calm and active children, some of us may be raising children who are strong-willed. Although this may sound like a negative description, I want to emphasize how strong-willed children are likely headed toward great achievement as adults. They have stamina, determination, and fortitude to support them through challenges. They will use these characteristics to get through law school, invent the next great technology, or build a successful business. Strong-willed individuals often contribute positively to our world, but they can bring more than their fair share of challenges to their parents. Remember, they are a gift, even when they exhaust you and require yet another creative solution.

When a strong-willed child becomes hostile, your goal is to avoid the agony of a push-pull power struggle. If you say no, they will say yes. If you tell them to stop, they will want to simply prove a point and engage their will. To redirect their desire to hit and strike out, the most effective strategy is to simply ask them questions and shift them from feeling to thinking. Here is an example. Your child is playing house with an older sibling. The older sibling is pretending to cook a meal and using all of the pots and pans. Your younger, strong-willed child decides they want to use one of the pans to give water to the dog. The whole scenario is now messed up from your older sibling's perspective, and the two of them get into an argument. The younger child becomes extremely frustrated and angry. You walk into the room just as your child is winding up to hit their sibling with the pan. "Hey! Why are you hitting your brother?" Your child will most likely have very few words. They are angry and full of emotion and may respond with a simple "because" or "he's mean." You can reply with, "Before you hit him (and you may need to physically get between the two of them if your child is very young), tell me about what happened." Your child will then outline their perspective. Let your older child know their turn will come. As your child shares their frustration, continue to ask questions: "Tell me more," or "How did that make you feel?" With the energy diffused, you can better support both of them in coming to a solution.

BITING

Sometimes children lash out at others by biting. This is another instinctual reaction to anger, frustration, and resentment. Bites hurt, so you want to deter children from using biting to express emotions. Similar to hitting, you need to act swiftly. Perhaps you can provide newspapers or scraps of paper to tear, or you can bring out those pillows. Take a few minutes to also comfort the person your child bit. This action will teach your child empathy and help them recognize the negative outcome of biting. Of course, ensuring your child isn't tired or hungry going into a playdate or heading to the playground supports their ability to manage emotions. If you are the one suffering from a bite, it may trigger a desire to lash out on your part as well. These are instances when you will have to dig deep and find patience. If you lash out, smack them, or bite back, it will only encourage bad behavior, and you will have shown them this type of hostility is an acceptable response.

Another strategy for strong-willed children is to simply find a way to physically separate them from the situation. Sometimes you will be in a place where this will work, but not always. In the previous example, you could also have entered the room and said, "Whoa, it looks like this is getting out of hand, so let's go downstairs and see if we can find the kitty." Most likely, you will experience resistance from your child, as they are full of anger and ready to lash out, so you will have to be creative and firm. "We can come back in a few minutes to finish this argument, but right now, you need to do something else." With the reassurance they can return to their revenge, they may be more willing to join you and go see the cat. Once some of the emotion has dissipated, return to the scene of the argument to resolve the issue. As parents, we often see an immediate solution to the problem at hand—share the pan, call the pan a water bowl, etc. However, if you are always the one to come up with a solution, your children won't have the opportunity to learn. Instead, when both children are a little calmer, ask them to come up with a way they can both play with the kitchen items amicably. You will be surprised at how resourceful and creative they can be in coming up with solutions. Additionally, they will be much more likely to follow through with their own idea rather than yours, and they will have had the opportunity to learn how to negotiate to solve a problem—a win-win situation.

Hostile Language

Some children are exceptionally verbal. They learn to talk at a young age and seem never to stop. As with all children, they are a gift to our families and the world. Their ability to verbalize can also come across as what some people would call sassy or talking back. They are learning how to use their skill, and it doesn't always go well. Remember, mistakes are the best way to learn, and although it is uncomfortable for adults, shutting down these children (or shutting them up) is not the answer. Your goal is to encourage the use of language in a way which will benefit the child and the world around them.

These children may lash out with both physical attacks and verbal attacks. An unsuspecting playmate won't know what hit them when they unleash their wrath.

To support these children in learning how to manage their anger and frustration, you will need to be quick. They will go from zero to sixty in a matter of minutes. Your best approach is to recognize their need for control. An example could be a preschool classroom where all of the children are sitting together listening to a story. A neighboring child reaches over and starts poking or disrupting. This annoyance causes our verbal child to become frustrated and angry, and they immediately turn to the troublemaker with fire in their eyes and clenched fists at their sides. If you see this initial response, it's time to step between them. Your best course of action is to keep the children apart and talk to them separately. I recommend taking your angered child to a quiet space free of distractions. You will find they will immediately calm down without the stimulation. Not only do their emotions escalate quickly, but they also de-escalate quickly. When they are calm, you can talk to them about what to do next time a similar situation happens. Remember, your verbal child can already process language more easily than their peers. Since you witnessed the interaction, you can offer your child alternatives to getting mad. Share with them how, when a friend is not listening, another option is to simply move away and sit with another friend. If the child is old enough, you can also explain how the friend simply wants some attention. You could advise your child to give them a smile or some other kind of acknowledgement.

This example reminds me of how our children's uniqueness can be challenging. When our child has a different personality or way of being from our own, it can be challenging to empathize and find creative solutions to support their learning rather than a quick punishment. In the previous example, it would have been easier to reprimand the child, telling them simply to stop raising their fists or they will have to go to time-out. Similarly, it can also be challenging to parent a child who has similar characteristics to you. They provide reminders of underlying traits we may not want to examine. Regardless of the situation, it is important to empathize with your child and recognize their strengths. Remember the list at the beginning of this chapter:

- A person's intention is always positive from their point of view.
- Everyone is doing the best they can at any moment, given their resources and their abilities.
- No child purposely misbehaves.

Imagine being the child in the previous example. Picture how annoying your friend poking you would feel. Then, when you respond with the only tools you have, an adult puts you into time-out. Instead of feeling supported, you are faced with yet another challenge. You can see how punishment produces more misbehavior. Rather than having an opportunity to address the feelings, children punished for incorrect behavior feel they are forced to bottle up their emotions and fume in time-out. In place of punishment, children need to learn better options for dealing with conflict, and they need adults to acknowledge their anger and frustration.

As with tantrums, preventing hostility is beneficial. As you watch your child play, you will learn to identify the early signs of anger and frustration. When you see these early signals, interject with guidance. Perhaps your child is playing with a new toy, one they cannot quite figure out. You see the frustration mounting as they repeatedly fail to get the toy to work. Some frustration is good—it drives innovation and determination—but when the frustration begins to transform into anger, it is helpful to support your child in managing the situation. In this example, you could first step in and name what is happening. "It looks like you are starting to get angry with the toy." Next, you can share some ideas. "When I start to feel angry, I like to take a break from what I'm doing because I know it will only make things worse to keep trying. Do you want to try taking a break?" Then, suggest some activities you know your child enjoys, such as sitting and reading a book together, playing with a favorite stuffed animal, or other cherished activities. Once your child is calmer, go back to the toy and guide them through how it works. Let them experiment with solutions too in order to demonstrate how problem-solving is easier when people are not angry.

Remember, when your child is hungry, ill, or tired, they will have even less control over their emotions. Asking your child to maintain composure in challenging situations, while also needing food, sleep, or healing time, only exacerbates the situation and increases the likelihood of frustration, anger, and hostility. Before meeting new friends or going on a play date with a friend who habitually challenges your children, make sure they have the resources they need.

"For the first time, the sweet infant who gazed lovingly into your eyes is questioning your word. What happened? It is not only maddening, but it also feels like betrayal."

RESISTANCE

In addition to managing the physical responses of tantrums and lashing out, toddlers are also learning about boundaries. Your two-, three-, or four-year-old may also react to boundaries and verbal requests with resistance or what looks like out right defiance. Phrases like, "How dare she get out of bed when I just told her she had to stay!" may go through your mind. It may feel as though your power and authority are being questioned, and you, too, may react from a place of defiance. Most likely, another power struggle is on the horizon. For the first time, the sweet infant who gazed lovingly into your eyes is questioning your word. What happened? It is not only maddening, but it also feels like betrayal. All those sleepless nights you endured—the feedings, the diaper changes—and this is how you are repaid? Okay, this example might be a little extreme, but feelings of loss and betrayal may surface as your infant, who is almost an extension of you, becomes a separate human with feelings, reactions, and a mind of their own.

Experiment

I remember having to get my children dressed some mornings when that was the last thing they wanted to do. In particular, one of my older daughters did not want to put on her tights—I called it "tights trauma." She needed the seams at the toes to be perfect, or the feeling would drive her crazy. The legs needed to be perfectly straight, and the waistband had to be even. My solution at the time was to basically power through it, practically wrestling her to the ground to get them on. In hindsight, I suspect a better solution was available. I could have skipped the tights all together, we could have put them on the night before, or I could have explored her ability to put them on herself. Because I approached raising my next two children without punishment, the battles were much fewer and farther between. It made a difference setting the stage early on for a balanced relationship. The trials you experience will be minimized when the push and pull of a power struggle is also minimized. Allowing your child to make age-appropriate choices about what they wear and when they get dressed can decrease resistance. If your child wants to sleep in their clothes, so they don't have to get up and dress, let them try it. If your night owl is a mess in the mornings, let them go to child care in their pajamas and change when they get there. Every situation is unique, but gradually supporting your child in finding their own morning routine is easier than forcing them to do things your way.

Movement

Another potential struggle arises when we need our toddlers to sit still. Perhaps it is a wedding, a religious ceremony, or a school play for an older child—any number of events where our young child has no intention of sitting still. They are ready to play! Several options are available to you in this instance, and many factors will contribute to how you approach the situation—the temperament of your child, your level of patience, the type of event, and your willingness to miss part of it. I remember taking one of my younger children to a movie with sisters when she was about three years old. I could see her starting to get restless while my two older children were engaged in the movie. Not wanting to ruin the film for everyone in the audience, I took her to an area at the back of the theater. She could play and move about without disturbing others, and I could peek around the corner to see what was happening onscreen. After a while, my husband came to spend time with her while I sat down and enjoyed the movie. Soon, our young child had expended some energy, and all three of us were back in our seats once again.

It is not always possible to give your child the opportunity to move about. Sometimes they really do need to sit quietly and stay with you. Finding something quiet for them to do is another option. I have often pulled a pen and a blank check out of my purse to keep a young child engaged. You can always void the check, and they will be engaged with drawing and exploring. If a child is old enough, give them a task. Ask them to count how many people fit in each row of the auditorium or how many blue items they can find on the stage. Parents often believe if they don't force their child to sit still at a young age with the use of threats and punishment, they will never learn to sit still. Remember my family's fear about how an unpunished child would end up running wild through the forest? I can tell you this fear is unfounded. As children mature and learn to better manage their emotions, they eventually are able to sit and enjoy their brother's play, their sister's band performance, or Aunt Suzy's wedding.

Safety

Sometimes a child's refusal to do what's asked puts them in harm's way. We cannot allow a child to run into the street or not sit safely strapped in their car seat. These are times when our lived experience takes precedence over a child's choice, opinion, or need to move about. In these instances, you need to be firm and loving. While it's not always easy to remain calm, you will not want to come across as angry. Any physical restraint should be only as firm as needed to buckle the car seat buckle or to swoop a child up into your arms. What follows next needs to be a consistent message for your child. Find a phrase that works well for you and your family. Perhaps it is something like, "Safety first!" or, "We need to keep ourselves safe!" This consistent message will support your child in learning how much you care about them and how your goal is to keep them safe, rather than maintain your authority. Keep it simple, and don't make a big deal out of it, even if it feels like a big deal to you. Seeing your child heading toward the street can cause your heart to miss a beat. However, if you make a big deal of it, your child may see this as a way to get your attention in the future. Minimize the event, so it doesn't become a point for future power struggles.

IMAGINATION

I wrote this book to support parents in guiding and educating their children as they grow and to help parents discover ways to address challenging behavior other than threats and punishment. However, I also want to include the joys of parenting. Parenting is a rewarding endeavor, and once you stop (or never start!) punishing, you will find that a rich relationship becomes available to you. During the toddler years, take time to enjoy your child's imagination and drive to play and explore. The information processing and logical parts of the brain are just beginning to develop, so most of what a young child experiences at this age is pure emotion, including joy. Learning how to play with a ball, seeing what happens when you drop a spoon from the highchair over and over, or sensing the different textures of blankets, carpets, grass, and other surfaces are fascinating to their young minds. This is an opportunity for you to tap into this part of yourself as well.

Take time to join your child when they are outside playing. Stop the chatter of your mind and truly experience the world around you. Find the joy they are feeling when they walk barefoot in the grass, feel the sand sift through their fingers, or squish the cookie dough with their hands. This is an opportunity for you to bring happiness into your busy life as the parent of an active toddler. We all want our children to live full, rich, and happy lives. The best way to ensure they experience these emotions is to model them. When you feel happiness, it spreads to them. You cannot give to anyone something you also do not feel.

CHAPTER 6:

YOUNG CHILDREN, AGES 5–9

NEXT, WE WILL EXPLORE the ages of about five to nine years old. When I ask people the ages of their children, I love to hear an answer in this range. Children at this stage are so full of life and amazing to be around. It is also a time for parents and children to bond and to really get to know one other another. Children in this age group love being with their parents, taking vacations, playing games, sharing secrets, and simply connecting. Parents are no longer lugging diaper bags around, buckling car seats, or having to be highly vigilant to keep toddlers safe. Some may call these years the salad days of parenting. It is also the time when your influence on your child is keenest. At this stage, you lay the important groundwork for their values, habits, and priorities, as your children will absorb these and begin to create a picture of themselves. The relationship you develop with your children at this time sets the stage for future relationships in their lives. They will grow accustomed to how they feel when they are with you and will seek out those same feelings in adulthood. It is your opportunity to create an environment that mirrors what you want for your child. Sow joy and happiness to reap a joyful adult. Minimize intolerance to create someone who is thoughtful and caring. Take a few minutes to read "Guidance for Parenting Young Children" and keep this information in mind to support your ever-deepening relationship with your child. This chapter focuses on parenting strategies for supporting sibling relationships, addressing dishonesty, and encouraging positive activities.

GUIDANCE FOR PARENTING YOUNG CHILDREN:

- A child learns more from your actions than your words.
- A child's primary goal is to connect with others, especially parents.
- When you honor your child's differences, they learn to honor differences in others.
- The adult relationships your child develops will reflect the relationship they have with you.
- How you treat your child, is how they will treat others.
- How you care for yourself impacts how you care for your child.

SIBLINGS

Not all of you will have more than one child, although your child may still engage with cousins or other family members who are near their age. Sibling fighting is one of the most common challenges parents will face. We love our children, so to see them at odds is disconcerting. Can't we all just get along? The family is the crucible for learning and growing. As hot ovens are able to mold and form metal, the intensity of our familial relationships molds and forms us. We would not want life to be all roses and chocolate; we need challenges to push us forward, support our growth, and mold us into our better selves.

Your Role

Sibling conflict is an important component of growing up with brothers, sisters, or cousins. Helping children learn how to negotiate conflict peacefully and appropriately is the job of parents, aunts, uncles, and grandparents. Several strategies are available and depend on the situation, temperaments of the children involved, and resources at hand (patience, time, and creativity). As you help children learn about conflict management and resolution, your role is to stay calm, nonjudgmental, and neutral. If you rush into the room yelling, frustrated with their fighting, it will only fuel the adversarial energy in the room. You will contribute to the conflict rather than help to resolve it. Confronting them with questions like "Who started this?" and, "What's going on here?" will only put them on the defensive, as they will have to negotiate their relationship with you as well as the struggle they are having with their sibling. Think of your position as the neutral umpire or referee in a sporting event. They are trained to be observant, not take sides, and bring a rational perspective in an environment rife with heated emotions and competitive drive. Your role is to bring a sense of calmness and to demonstrate problem-solving. With some creativity, you can resolve the conflict and reinforce how the relationship is more important than the issue at hand. Before walking into the room, take a few deep breaths and go in with awareness of your role, rather than responding from the natural inclination to yell and threaten.

Focus on Behavior

In teaching your children to resolve conflict, or at least to address it with civility, focus on the behavior and the issue, not the individuals. We are not raising "bad" children or "good" children. These labels only make the situation worse, even if they are only in your head. Additionally, we typically don't find someone who is right and someone who is wrong; it's usually only a misunderstanding, conflict, argument, or disagreement. Let's walk through a scenario of two children fighting over what to watch on television. You may walk in to see them wrestling over the remote, yelling at each other about whose turn it is to pick the movie or show. You see immediately they are both angry, righteous, and determined to get their way. Your first instinct may be to yell, "Stop fighting!" but remember, if you yell and get angry, you will fuel the argument, rather than help to resolve it. Instead, calmly step between them, hold out your hand, and ask for the remote. You will be surprised at how quickly the energy begins to dissipate. They will shout out justifications and rationalizations for why they should get the remote versus their sibling but assure them you will listen to both perspectives. Let each of them have a voice and listen intently, providing feedback to indicate you understand what they are saying. They need to feel heard and appreciated for their opinions. Then tell them they both have strong arguments, but it is important to come to a resolution. Ask them if either of them has an idea for how the issue can be solved to address both of their needs. How can they decide what to watch in a way that will support them both? You will be amazed at how creative your children can be. As they shift their attention to problem-solving, their frustration and anger will dissipate even more. They will also feel heard, so their frustration will also diminish. You will have created an environment where they (and you) can be patient, creative, and resourceful in figuring out a resolution. Most of the time, my children came up with great solutions; I was often amazed at how they could take a black-and-white situation and find a gray area. If your children struggle, or they come up with a solution where one of them is compromising more than the other, then it is appropriate to offer ideas. What if we watch one of your movies today, and as a family, we watch the other movie after dinner? What if one of you watches your show on the television, and we get out the headphones and my iPad for the other to watch theirs? Ensure both children feel that the solution works. After a few times of working with your children, they will soon learn how to negotiate with each other before emotions turn ugly.

"Siblings often misbehave because they are looking for attention, either from you or their peers."

Now, let's look at this same scenario using punishment as the solution. This time, you walk into the room yelling. You grab the remote away from them and say, "I am so tired of listening to the two of you fight! Nobody is watching TV! Now go to your rooms, and I don't want to see or hear anything from either of you for the next hour!" That approach is quick and effective, and you are able to get right back to preparing dinner. Whew! But what will your children learn? Do you think they will go back to their rooms and think about how to resolve conflict better? No! They will go to their rooms fuming, thinking about how unfair you are and how next time, they will be even more aggressive and mean to their sibling in order to get what they want. Their anger and frustration will have escalated. They will have learned about the negative aspects of hierarchy and power—whoever is bigger is in charge and gets to mete out the punishment and make the decisions. They will not have learned how to manage conflict, control their emotions, or solve problems. I used an extreme example to prove a point, but many parents don't think about their options and often respond with what comes naturally (or how they were parented)—elevated emotions and lashing out.

Provide Attention

Siblings often misbehave because they are looking for attention, either from you or their peers. This often appears as teasing or picking on another. Sometimes it is in an older sibling bothering a younger one, or sometimes the younger one antagonizes the older one. Boys may tease girls, and girls may prod and poke at boys. Siblings and cousins find many ways to ridicule each other. To be clear, not every form of teasing is harmful, and different individuals and families have different thresholds. Some families razz and tease as a form of endearment, but other times the teasing is clearly unwanted and creates animosity. I remember how my friend would incessantly tickle me as a young child. She thought it was wonderful to be able to trigger such a consistent and annoying reaction in me. I hated it. I also remember my first two daughters struggling because the younger was active and wanted to play, but if her older sister didn't respond, she would start kicking or hitting her to get her attention. These are a couple of examples of how siblings may not actually be fighting, but their behavior may still make some parents want to end it quickly with a threat or punishment. "Stop bugging your sister, or I'll take your phone away for a week."

In most of these circumstances, the tormentor's intentions are not evil; they simply want to evoke a response and feel connected to the other person. Your approach to these situations can set the stage for the future of the relationship. Helping your children create healthy relationships with their siblings is a gift they will appreciate later in life. You may recall from an earlier chapter the role-playing exercise where one participant pretends to be a child with a beautiful stone to show to their parent. If the "child" is ignored, they will be persistent in the attempt to get the attention of the "parent." If the "parent" takes a few moments to acknowledge the beautiful stone, the "child" will feel recognized and will go back to playing. You can share this same strategy with your children. Help them understand that each of us wants to feel heard and appreciated, and ensuring everyone has a voice can go a long way in creating more harmony in your family.

To illustrate what this looks like, let's take the example of my two daughters. When I noticed my younger daughter kicking her sister, rather than repeatedly telling her to stop and threatening her with punishment, I could have taken a different approach. Notice how it had to be repeated—the punishment reinforced the negative behavior. Another approach I could have taken would have been to name what I observed and support them in understanding how the situation had unfolded. I could have asked my younger daughter, "Are you kicking your sister because you want her attention?" The question would have probably caught her off guard, but more than likely it would have caused her to pause for a minute. "Is there another way for you to get her attention?" Through this strategy, I would have also had the older daughter's attention. "Although your sister appears to be annoying right now, she really just wants someone to play with. Can you two have a conversation about when you might be able to do something together? I can see you are busy right now, but perhaps you could plan to play soccer in the yard or play a video game together once you are done with the chapter in your book?" Support both of your children in having their needs met. Asking one to drop whatever they are doing to attend to the needs of the other is not helpful as the one needing attention will become a burden. Once again, you will find your children can be quite creative in resolving these issues. In this example, it would also have been helpful if I had stepped in and found something to do with my younger daughter—giving her some mother/daughter time while she was feeling restless. With a plan to spend some time with her sister later in the day, she would have felt heard.

This example provides a window into my "grand experiment." The scenario I described reflected traditional parenting—using punishment to stop misbehavior. With my two experimental children, this type of situation rarely, if ever, came up. Because both of them felt respected, empowered, valued, and appreciated, it was a rare occurrence when they felt the need to tease or pick on each other. Looking back, I see this example as evidence of how punishment is not only an unnecessary component of raising children, but it also contributes to disharmony and frustration.

~~~~~~~~~~

"Brain experts have found that somewhere around four or five years of age, a lightbulb goes on in children's brains."

~~~~~~~~~~

DISHONESTY
Lying

I am definitely intrigued by this topic. We experience white lies, protective lies, cruel lies, and unintended lies. My opinion on dishonesty has changed over the years. When I was young, I remember my mother telling white lies to her mother, my grandmother. She would tell me how we didn't want to upset grandma, and sometimes it was better for my grandmother not to know about specific situations. Somewhere in my late twenties or early thirties, I realized lying actually takes hard work. I had to remember who I told what lies to. I decided to stop lying, and it was quite freeing. When I caught people lying in my life, I would be disappointed and consider it a failing on their part. Recently, in becoming more observant of human nature, I have concluded that oftentimes, *we* are the reason other people lie. We back them into a corner or put them into an awkward situation where they feel compelled to lie to protect themselves or the relationship. Lying is fascinating.

Brain experts have found that somewhere around four or five years of age, a lightbulb goes on in children's brains. Prior to this time, a child's understanding of the world is quite literal. They accept that what is happening around them is apparent to everyone. Even if a parent is not in sight, they assume that parent is all-knowing. They incorrectly believe that because they know something, their parent knows it as well. When that light bulb goes on—when their brain develops into higher levels of thinking—they realize that what their parents and other people know may be different than what they know. They realize you won't know if they are playing with blocks behind a closed door instead of getting dressed. This positive and important stage in development—the ability to recognize differences in "knowing"—is also the key to learning how to lie.[25] It is an important milestone. However, you want them to use this new skill appropriately and not for lying. Here are three tactics to help your child learn to be honest:

- Be creative with your responses; turn it into a game.
- Reframe your questions; ensure you are not backing them into a corner.
- Use observation; address the issue without accusation.

Be Creative

The first time your child lies should be a celebration—one you probably want to keep to yourself. When your child is young and begins to start lying, make a game of it. Let's picture what this might look like. Your four-year-old has just told their first lie. You asked them to put their blocks back into the bin when they were done playing. Later, they come into your office and ask to go to the park. You ask, "Did you put your blocks in the bin?" They look to the left, then back at you, and say, "Yes!" However, when you walk upstairs to get their shoes, you see blocks scattered all over the bedroom. Like most people, your first sensation is likely one of betrayal. How dare they! However, remember we are raising kids who are still learning to navigate the world. They don't yet have the skillset to even think about betrayal. They are experimenting with how the world works. What happens if I tell Mom and Dad what they want to hear, even if it isn't exactly what happened? The challenge here is to respond intentionally, not instinctually. Responding with anger and betrayal will only confuse your child. They won't understand why you're mad.

In place of an instinctual response, let's get creative. Turn to your child and observe, "Wow. I still see blocks on the floor of your room." State the evidence without judgement. Your child may look a little sheepish and confused. Give them an opportunity to right their wrong, rather than be punished. "How about if we make it a game? Let's see who can pick up the most blocks." You will be spending some quality time with your child, and they will experience forgiveness, rather than punishment. When you identified the reality of the situation, you clearly stated what they told you was inaccurate. Then you supported them in the process of making it right. The experience will likely leave them feeling more connected to you, not hurt and angry, and they will be less likely to lie to you again.

If we look at this same situation with a typical knee-jerk reaction, the outcome is different. You look into the room and see the blocks. You respond from anger, turning to your child and condemning them. "You lied to me about the blocks! How dare you! Lying is wrong, and you are bad. Now go into your room, clean up those blocks immediately, and you're grounded for the rest of the day! No park for you!" More than likely, this response will stun your child. They had no idea their action would create such a response. They will feel guilty, hurt, and unfairly punished. Evidence shows most children will respond with, "Next time I won't get caught. I'll show them!"

Reframe Questions

If you find that your child consistently lies to you, it is time to take stock of your relationship with them. My experience working with people in a variety of settings, including family members, is that each person is doing the best they can at any given moment considering their current knowledge and resources. If someone is lying to you, you may need to consider the questions you are asking or the requests you are making. We will explore teenagers in a future chapter, but for this age group, five to nine years old, lying can be correlated to the incongruence of expectations from you as a parent and their ability (or interest) to align with those expectations. As an example, you may believe strongly in the importance of playing youth sports. You have always loved athletic activity, and you have read about the positive outcomes of good physical health and teamwork. Your child, on the other hand, may not be as inclined to this type of activity. Their temperament might be driven toward other types of activities such as dance, yoga, or simple walks. When you insist your child lives up to your ideals or interests—even though they simply cannot find the same passion—you will be setting up a situation where they will either consistently resist and argue, or they will begin to lie in order to keep you happy.

Use Observation

Another example of a situation where children fall into a pattern of lying is when we ask pointed questions with negative accusations built in. Sometimes, without thinking, we set up our child to either feel terrible about themselves or to lie. Perhaps your child has had a wonderful experience playing in the rain with a favorite raincoat and galoshes. The activity has filled them with joy, and they come running into the house to share their delight. In the heat of the moment, they not only forget to close the door behind them, but they also track mud down the hallway. Later in the day, you see the muddy hallway and know who created the mess. You go to your child and ask, "Did you forget again to take off your boots and get mud all over my nice clean hallway?" Who wants to respond to that question? Depending on your child's temperament, they may feel awful, admit to the error, and apologize. Another child might try to defend their position with outlandish stories. "I had to, Mom. A dog was chasing me, and I was scared!" Another child might try to lie their way out of the scenario. "I didn't see the mud on my boots," or, "It must have been my little sister. I didn't do it."

"You will have shared your own needs, and will have given your child an opportunity to restore the situation and maintain their sense of worth."

When you know a child has made a mistake, rather than ask accusatory questions, it is better to simply address the issue straight on. In this example, you could approach your child with, "Hey, I saw you came in from playing in the rain with muddy boots." Your child now has the opportunity to respond with, "Yes. It was great fun. How did you know?" You will be able to respond further with, "I saw mud in the hallway. I like to keep the hallway clean. Let's go downstairs, and we can clean it up together while you tell me more about playing in the mud." You will accomplish several positive outcomes with this response. You will have addressed the issue without making your child feel poorly about their behavior. You will have shared your own needs, and will have given your child an opportunity to restore the situation and maintain their sense of worth. You will not have backed them into a corner from which they are likely to lie.

Stealing

In addition to lying, parents also want to ensure their children don't cheat or steal. These behaviors are not common with children this age, but you may find yourself with a child who inadvertently or unwittingly takes something from a store, a friend's house, or a family member without thinking about the consequences. Candy and gum in the checkout aisle at the store are attractive to most young children. Parents of these youngsters may arrive home to find a candy bar in their child's pocket for which they didn't pay. When these situations happen, it is important to share your family's values with your child and ensure they don't end up behind bars as adults; however, this situation doesn't require a severe response. In almost all cases, the stealing is not intentional, nor is it premeditated. Addressing it directly, kindly, and compassionately will go a long way in preventing further accidental shoplifting.

When you discover the stolen property, you will want to address the situation as quickly as possible. As with lying, don't back your child into a corner with accusatory questions such as, "Did you steal this candy from the store?!?" You know you didn't pay for the candy, so the question is not necessary. Simply state the obvious. "I see you have some candy, and I did not pay for it. We need to pay for everything we get from the store, including this candy. We need to take it back and tell the store manager you made a mistake." At this point, you will have several options. Often, parents will have the child apologize to the store manager. Some parents will have the child use an allowance to go back to the store and pay for it. Others may make sure the child understands the situation and will then dispose of the candy. This is a good time to remind readers that I don't intend to tell you specifically how to parent. I want to provide insights into all the options you have to consider. Each parent-child relationship is unique, even within the same family. Part of being a supportive parent is working to be in tune with your child and recognizing what works best for them.

Cheating

You may also run into a situation where your child is cheating. It may be in a game, on a test at school, or in negotiations with friends and siblings. A child cheats because they feel they need to live up to an expectation to always win. A household that puts pressure on family members to always be the best or excel may be setting up their children to feel it is okay to cheat because the end justifies the means. Remember, there is a difference between encouraging your child to do *their* best and telling your child they must be *the* best. No one can be the best at everything, and creating an environment where a child feels they need to constantly excel creates undue pressure and hardship, to the point where they may feel compelled to cheat.

When you discover your child is cheating, it is important to address it. Making your way through life with a habit of cheating leads to a variety of hardships, both in external relationships and with one's own health and well-being. Let's look at an example. Your nine-year-old is playing a game with two friends, and the goal is to collect cards. You see your child sneak cards from their pocket, planted there before the game. Once the friends have gone home, find some time to discuss what you saw. You already know not to use an accusatory question such as, "Did you cheat!?!?" This approach will put your child on the defense, incite feelings of guilt, and make it challenging to have an effective conversation about the situation. Simply and kindly state what you saw. "Hey, I saw you slip some cards from your pocket during the game. Tell me more about what was going on." Let your child express their perspective and explain how they were feeling then help them understand how their feelings negatively affected their actions. You might respond with, "I understand you wanted to win, and for the last few times your friends came over, you lost every time. Losing does feel bad, so I can see why you were so anxious to win this time." Your tone should be loving and supportive. "However, let's think about how you would feel if you found out one of your friends won because they cheated. It doesn't feel great, and it spoils the game for everyone. I want you and your friends to enjoy playing the game and not worry so much about winning and losing, as long as you're having fun together. Maybe next time your friends come over, you can do some different activities—games without winners and losers. You could take our dog for a walk, have a scavenger hunt, or build something. Do you have ideas of what might be fun for the three of you?" Make sure your child knows you are in their corner, ready to help them figure out how to enjoy time with their friends. Involve them in the problem-solving and let them know cheating is not okay, but they are still okay. They are not a bad person; they simply made a mistake.

"Putting a child in time-out, grounding them, or taking away privileges to enforce your message only creates separation and disconnection."

At the beginning of this chapter, the list of guidance included "A child's primary goal is connection to others, especially parents." When you discover your child has explored lying, cheating, or stealing as options to address a problem, you will want to ensure you explore the conflict and maintain your connection with them. Your response should encourage collaborative problem-solving, rather than contribute to an adversarial relationship. Staying connected to you and valuing the relationship will be the supportive foundation not only this time, but also as they move into preteen and teenage years. Putting a child in time-out, grounding them, or taking away privileges to enforce your message only creates separation and disconnection. Remember the exercise when I asked you to recall a time when you were punished? Punishment rarely feels justified, and what we remember is our own frustration and anger, not the lesson our parents intended us to learn. Your children don't wake up in the morning with bad intentions. However, because they are inexperienced at living in our world, they can make mistakes such as lying, cheating, and stealing. Support them in identifying these actions as mistakes, and show them other options. Finally, ensure you model a lifestyle with minimal negative behaviors.

POSITIVE ACTIVITIES

In addition to teaching our children what not to do (lie, cheat and steal), we also need to teach them what *to* do. We need to guide them as they learn to navigate our world. This section discusses strategies on how to support children in becoming contributing, respectful members of our society.

Household Contributions

Let's begin with contributions around the house, sometimes referred to as chores. I like to say contribution because "chore" sounds like, well, a chore. It has a negative connotation. When children are very young, usually around the age of three years old, you can't keep them out from under your feet. They want to help you clean, cook, and tidy the yard. They are curious and want to participate in everything you do, hence the plastic lawnmowers, kitchen sets, and gardening tools available in the toy aisle. However, once your child gets a little older, this fascination ends, and their desire shifts to exploring their own world of friends, games, sports, books, etc. Getting them to help out around the house can become a little more challenging. From my experience, this topic showed some of the greatest differences among my four children. Some of them contributed naturally—they liked having a clean room, messing around in the kitchen during dinner, unloading the dishwasher without being asked… You get the picture. Others were not at all interested in these types of activities. They preferred rooms with a little more clutter, were highly engaged in academics, and only helped out when asked—it didn't come naturally for them. For the record, it didn't matter if they were part of the control group or if they were my experimental children. I had a child in each group who easily engaged with housework and one who struggled more.

As with most of what we have discussed in this book, each child will respond differently to your attempts to engage them with contributing around the house. I recommend working closely with them and capitalizing on their strengths. Watch to see what they enjoy doing—where their interests lie. If they are animal lovers, helping out with the family pets is the best way for them to contribute. If they are creative and like to experiment, the kitchen is often the best place for them. If they love the outdoors and highly physical activities, get them outside to help with yard work. Each family has to determine if contributing around the house is simply what you all do or if these activities earn an allowance or payment. In our home, we did a little of both. Some regular chores (feeding the animals) were contributions we expected; for more involved projects (helping to install a fence), we paid our children for their contribution. No answer is right or wrong; you need to determine what works best for your family and your children. Take a few minutes to read "Household Contributions (Chores)."

Steer away from using rewards or punishments to motivate your child to contribute. You want them to be intrinsically motivated to help around the house. Rather than saying, "You can't go to Jamil's house until you sweep out the garage," it would be more effective to talk about what's needed around the house on Sunday night and say, "Our garage really needs to be swept out and I could use some help. Who wants to help with this project?" If no one steps up, you could say, "I like to have the garage neat, so we can all find what we need. I really need one of you to help." Once someone agrees, find a suitable time and have them make a commitment. When the time comes to complete the task, you can remind them. Ideally, you have set up a time when you can both go out to the garage to work on it together. You can organize the tools while your child sweeps. If a playdate comes up during the same time, renegotiate a time to work on the garage. Using the playdate or another activity as a reward or punishment that is associated with the housework will link a negative feeling with contributing. The contribution will become the barrier to doing what they love, and you will have set the stage for resistance.

HOUSEHOLD CONTRIBUTIONS (CHORES)

The ideal way to support a child in learning to contribute around the house is to give them plenty of input and choice. Here are some tips:

- If you dictate the activities, you will more than likely run into resistance.
- Collaborate with children to determine their activities, and they will be more engaged.
- Mix up the work. We all get tired of repetitive chores.
- Have a rotating schedule of activities. For example, they can do yard work for the first and third weekends of the month and housecleaning for the second and fourth.
- Model the work. When they see you contributing, they recognize it is something we all do.
- Work together. When you join in, they'll be more engaged.

Keep family contributions separate from other activities. Rather than saying, "If you clean your room, you can have three hours of video games," try, "Let's set some time aside on Thursdays to spend one hour on your room." Keep the time limit reasonable based on age and temperament. For some children, ten minutes might be the best way to start; for older children or children with a focused temperament, it can be longer. Help them out initially, making a game of who can get the most done in an hour, or "shooting baskets" to get the blocks into the tub. Once you have reached the agreed upon time, stop. Getting the room perfectly clean is not important. What is important is the two of you working together on a family contribution and your child experiencing the positive results of their time investment. As your child matures and gets into the routine of spending some time on these tasks, your involvement will not be as essential.

I have one final piece on chores and taking responsibility for household contributions. Your child has an innate drive to be part of a thriving family. When you allow them to explore their gifts, interests, and desires, they will find ways to contribute. For some, it might be cooking. Others might despise the kitchen. Forcing a child to do a certain chore will only create tension and, eventually, resistance, which you will need to meet with stronger levels of threats and punishments to force compliance. You only have your children with you for a short time, and any parent with adult children will tell you to treasure the time you have with them because it will be over before you know it. You can spend your time with them in cooperative engagement or embroiled in power struggles. The choice is yours.

School Work

School work is another power struggle in some families. Most children five to nine years old still find great joy in spending their days with school friends and teachers. This is the time to ensure your child sees their education as something belonging to them, not you. You want to instill a sense of ownership in them. To begin, it is good to talk about school as a family. You can bring up the topic at the dinner table, while gathered to watch something on television, or on a family hike. Ask your child to share something good from their day at school, as well as one bad thing. Reminding your child that they will experience challenges along with their positive experiences is important. Ensure they know they have the support to meet those challenges, and then celebrate the good things.

Let's look at some examples. First, we'll use the example of a good grade. Your child has done well on a test. Let them know they should be proud of themselves. You can voice your own pride but focus on theirs. Talk about how they prepared and why they think they did well. Did they spend time ahead of the test going over the material? Did they talk with classmates about what was going to be on the test? Did they have good attendance, ensuring they didn't miss any of the information? Bringing awareness to these positive behaviors will support them in being a good student. Encouraging them to feel proud of themselves will instill a sense of ownership. You may also say how you are happy for them and share in their accomplishment. I recognize some families have a practice of paying their children for good grades or providing rewards. I would recommend not using this tactic or else minimizing it as much as possible, as it suggests learning does not bear its own reward and satisfaction. Happy adults are intrinsically motivated to learn and participate in professional growth. Encourage your child to relish the feeling of a job well done.

~~~~~~~~~~~~~~~~~~~~~~~~~~~

"To set an expectation in your home for everyone to perform perfectly all the time is a recipe for disaster."

~~~~~~~~~~~~~~~~~~~~~~~~~~~

Let's look at how to engage with your child if they receive a not-so-good grade. You need to make sure you have created an environment where your child feels it is safe to talk about poor performance. We all have times when the content simply doesn't sink in or we have been sick, or we simply make a mistake. To set an expectation in your home for everyone to perform perfectly all the time is a recipe for disaster. Share your mistakes and bad days, and make sure they know they can share theirs. A bad grade or poor performance feels bad enough, and it is even tougher if your child feels they can't talk about it. When your child reports they have performed poorly on a school assignment, your response should be empathetic and supportive. If you come across as disapproving and judgmental, you won't hear about future struggles. If your child is ready to discuss the situation, it is important to make sure they do most of the talking. This is not the time for a lecture on how to be a good student. Help your child put the grade into perspective. Have them recall other assignments where they have done well. Do they know why they performed poorly on this particular assignment? Spend a few minutes discussing the assignment, make sure they have a plan for how to do better next time, and move on. Make sure they know they are not alone in two ways. First, others (probably you) have performed poorly, and it is not shameful. Second, they can always reach out for help if needed—from you, their teacher, or online resources. Punishing your child for poor school performance is unnecessary; most of our schools provide ample feedback on poor performance.

What do you do if you have a child who is a chronic underperformer or if you suspect your child may struggle with learning due to a cognitive difference (learning disability)? This is an opportunity to support your child in learning how to live and grow through challenges. Your child will one day be an adult, and they will face many challenges throughout their life. Some may be quite positive—running a marathon, completing an advanced degree—and some may be not so positive—addressing a serious health concern or being in a stressful relationship. It is important to help our children learn to not only survive in challenging times, but also to thrive.

Several strategies are available if your child needs a little extra support:

- "Chunk" the information into smaller sections.
- Ensure adequate support is available at school.
- Avoid power struggles.
- Encourage study groups and engaging with friends.

Taking a problem or task and breaking it down into smaller chunks is one method. If your child brings home a math worksheet filled top to bottom with challenging math problems, use another piece of paper to cover up everything but the first row. It won't look so daunting, and your child may feel like the task is something they can accomplish. Encourage them to take a break, go outside, or play with a family pet once the row is complete. Then cover up all the problems except for the second row, and work on only that row. Your child could use the same strategy for writing. Writing intimidates some individuals, especially when the assignment must be of a specific length. Talk to your child about the project and help them to make the project manageable by setting goals. Take on only the introduction, or maybe the topic sentence. Once your child begins the process, as with taking a single bite of a new food, the pump will be primed, and they will likely be able to continue working.

In working with cognitive differences, ensure your child is also getting the support they need at school. The field of managing individual learning needs has grown, and experts are available in all school districts. These professionals have the tools needed to support students with a variety of skills and strengths. Your role is to help your child understand that it is okay to ask for help, and everyone has unique strengths and limitations. While one child may excel in creative endeavors, another may excel in science. Others may have prowess on the sports field, while some demonstrate a passion for working with young children. Point out your child's strengths and encourage them to recognize how everyone needs help in some areas of life. Being able to ask for help in the classroom is a strength, not a weakness.

Another strategy for helping children who struggle with schoolwork is to ensure their homework does not become one of your power struggles. Threats, rewards, and arguments will only deteriorate your relationship and create more negative energy around the homework or school work. Replace these irritants with love and support. Let your child share their frustrations and struggles so they feel heard, and let them know everyone has to go to school and complete the work. You can be firm with your expectations, while still ensuring they feel heard and supported.

In addition to breaking a hard task down into smaller chunks, you can also create a game for getting the work done. An example would be a social studies project where your child needs to fill in a map with the countries and color it in. Cut up small pieces of paper and write a country on each piece. Put the pieces into a bowl and have your child pull one out. The country listed on the paper is the first to find. Have them draw another, and so on. You will need to put on your creative hat to support your children, but once the drudgery and power struggles are set aside, homework will flow much more easily.

Some children benefit from study groups. These are common in college, but the concept works well at any age, especially if you have a social child. Being around friends can actually increase productivity for some children when they are all working on the same project. They can encourage each other and help to answer questions. Not every strategy will work for every child. However, I suspect you are getting a good sense of how to support a child who "doesn't like" school. Many children love school and will complete their work without any intrusion from you. Let their autonomy thrive and let school be their domain. If you still feel tempted to step in and help, remember you won't be there in high school and college. They will need to develop skills to manage schoolwork. If they are engaged, completing the work, and getting along with teachers, your job is to stand back and celebrate their successes with them!

School is a major part of your child's life during this age range. It will consume most of their day and some of their evenings. Nothing has greater potential to create joy, or strife. How you approach the early challenges will set the stage for your relationship with your child for several years to come. I was fortunate to have children who loved school or at least found it to be a positive experience. I also sent all my children to public Montessori charter schools, and there was an alignment with most of their teachers and the concepts in this book. The ultimate message for you is that schoolwork and classroom policies will provide the necessary discipline to guide your children. You do not need to add additional punishment or reprimands, nor do you need to reward them. Let the joy of learning be its own reward.

"If children feel forced to comply by simply mimicking words, they won't learn the true spirit of kindness that is necessary for developing positive relationships."

Graciousness

The final section under the topic on positive activities is about support-ing your child in what my grandmother would have referred to as "good manners." In our family, everyone discovered the importance of showing gratitude, asking for things graciously, and respecting the dignity of others. I believe a fine line exists between forcing a child to say "please" and "thank you" and supporting them in truly feeling these emotions. I have recollections of parents who have sternly said to their children, "What do you say?" with a tone of authority, illustrating their need for approval rather than considering the needs of their child. If children feel forced to comply by simply mimick-ing words, they won't learn the true spirit of kindness that is necessary for developing positive relationships.

To support our children in learning to be gracious, they need to see you and other adults communicating with each other with kindness. At the dinner table, model the behavior by using "please" and "thank you" when you talk to your partner and your children, and be sincere as often as you can. I can remember imploring one of my children, "*Please* don't make me ask you again to take out the trash." In addition to these hopefully infre-quent pleas, use respectful language when asking your child to contribute around the house or to help you out. It is worth repeating. Children will do what you do, not what you say. If they see you being kind to others, such as speaking respectfully even when you are frustrated in a customer service situation, they will adapt the same approach. Staying calm, being respectful, and looking for solutions will go a long way in creating a healthy and happy adulthood. People are much more willing to find solutions to problems if the person on the other end of the phone or chat can remain calm, rather than becoming angry.

You can also support your child in learning to be gracious in the moment, in ways other than a stern, "What do you say?" When we publicly reprimand with this phrase, children begin to associate saying "please" and "thank you" as a negative experience rather than as positive growth. Some children may even blush with embarrassment when confronted with this phrase in the presence of another adult. Alternatively, work with your child ahead of time to come up with a signal you can use to remind them. Maybe it's a smile and a wink of the eye to remind them to express their gratitude or ask graciously. Maybe you can say something such as, "We appreciate what you've done," which will prompt your child to enthusiastically say, "Yes! Thank you very much!" In this scenario, your child will learn to feel gratitude and respond naturally. Additionally, they will experience a sense of unity from you, which will support a trusting relationship.

A side note on the topic of graciousness that I have observed in some instances where parents ask children to say "please" and "thank you" more often than the adults around them. These children find themselves in a situation where it feels awkward because they are saying these words so frequently. In these environments, the words will simply become tools to get what they want, not expressing the intended expression of graciousness and gratitude. Before requiring your child to say "please," ask yourself, *"If I were in this situation with another adult, would I use the word "please"?"* As adults, we ask our family members or coworkers for help many times throughout the day. Sometimes we include the word "please," and other times we don't. Overuse begins to minimize the value of the word; it becomes mundane rather than a true expression of graciousness. The same is true, of course, for "thank you." When we say it, we should truly want to express our gratitude for what someone has done for us or for the gift they have given us.

One of the greatest gifts you can give your child is understanding the power of appreciation and gratitude. Along with love, feeling and expressing gratitude brings joy and happiness to a life well lived. Support your child in learning about how it feels to do good, live honestly, share with others, and connect with you and the rest of your family. These true gifts of childhood—not toys, games, or material things—are the early foundation that brings joy to our lives and promotes the internal spirit of peace.

In this chapter, we talked about supporting children ages five to nine years old. We explored how to support their relationships with siblings and other children, address dishonesty, and encourage participation in the household and school. Finally, we talked about appreciation and gratitude. In the next chapter, we'll explore preteens.

CHAPTER 7:

PRETEENS, AGES 10–14

WHEN OUR CHILDREN HIT DOUBLE DIGITS, they begin to transform. I have heard parents cry foul, "Who stole my child and left me with this alien?" The child who loved to snuggle or wanted to be with you all weekend now has other interests, friends who are important to their development, and a new brain. This was the age when I started to see a difference in my "experimental" children. Our relationship did not become strained, and they appeared to be more comfortable with the changes they experienced. Punishment-free parenting brings about an open heart, a sense of personal safety, and the confidence to live fully in childhood and young adulthood. Take a few minutes to read the "Guidance for Parenting Preteens," and then we'll take a look at my experience using punishment-free parenting through the preteen years. This chapter includes information on the importance of friends at this age, ideas on how to support children in learning about time management, and strategies to address challenges in their lives.

GUIDANCE FOR PARENTING PRETEENS

- They are experiencing a new sense of self, one influenced by new hormones.
- They still need your love and support, even if they don't always reciprocate it.
- Independence is a positive trait. You want your child to feel safe venturing into the world.
- Emotions run high, and they may be experiencing some of them for the first time.

The first ten years of your parenting approach will influence your experience with your preteen child. If you previously chose to maintain a punishment-free environment during the early years, this age range will be easier. If you previously incorporated punishment into your discipline philosophy, you will begin to see more negative outcomes during this time. In this chapter, we'll explore a variety of topics, and with each one, we will discuss some of the differences parents will see based on their approaches to discipline. This is where my "grand experiment" began to show some results. Where my control children pushed back, standing up for their rights and arguing consistently, my experimental children went into these years peacefully. They got along with each other better, were more cooperative, and had healthier relationships. It wasn't without a few bumps, but I could really see how creating a supportive environment without the threat of punishment gave them the strength, confidence, and peace of mind to approach the challenges of the preteen years with a more positive outlook.

No one gets up in the morning and states their intent for misbehavior or disobedience, but young people who live in a punitive environment wake up each morning wondering if they are going to get into trouble. Will they say the wrong thing? Do the wrong thing? Or worse yet, will they get caught? They are on guard most of the time, suspicious of the adults around them, and they either walk on egg shells or interact with defiance. In addition to naturally becoming more independent, they are feeling a sense of wanting to escape or get away. They start counting how many years they need to live at home, longing for the time they can get out from under the tyranny. You and your children probably fall somewhere in between the experience of peaceful preteen years and the environment I just described. Our children respond in unique ways to the influences of the world and our parenting. There is always hope. Even if you have grounded your preteen every weekend for the last six weeks, or if their cell phone spends more time in your nightstand drawer than their pocket, opportunities exist to repair the relationship. You know my perspective—these strategies don't work. Many of you may put this book down right now, vowing it is impossible to raise a preteen or teenager without punishment, but I am here to say it is not only doable, but it's also worth it. Stay with me as we dive into what a punishment-free adolescence looks like.

"Your role as parent and your style of parenting should not only be unique for each child, but it should also change and evolve along with your child."

FRIENDS

Developmentally, these are the years when your child begins to focus less on parents and more on friends. Whether it's sleep overs, afternoons participating in sports, or hanging out at a library or coffeeshop, your preteen is more engaged with their friends than ever before. Although it may be challenging to no longer be the center of their world, you should celebrate this developmental milestone. Your first inclination may be to hold them back, keep them close, and limit their time with friends. If you have been paying attention up until now, you know this desire for control only creates power struggles between you and your child. As long as your preteen is safe at a friend's house or a public space, letting them explore their world is the best thing you can do for them. These years are the bridge between childhood and adulthood. However, your child won't simply cross the bridge in a single trip, which can be challenging for a parent. They will venture part way out, spend some time there, and come back to the childhood space to build up confidence. They will then venture out again, maybe a little further, to see what the world holds. When friends cause painful emotions, or they feel confused, they will take a few steps back. Your job is to be there when they need you and support them in spreading their wings when they're ready. It is challenging because their needs most likely won't line up with yours. You may long for some snuggle time on the couch as they are heading out the door. Conversely, you may become accustomed to having a little more time for yourself, right when they walk in with tears, needing your comfort. Your role as parent and your style of parenting should not only be unique for each child, but it should also change and evolve along with your child. The evolution of a child into a preteen requires parental flexibility.

Your preteen's emotions now revolve more around their friends than their home life. Their friends will bring them their greatest joy but also their greatest pain. Preteens often learn some of the realities of relationships during these years. They will more than likely experience the positive emotions of connection, support, trust, and commitment. They will also experience the negative emotions of betrayal, animosity, and sadness. As your child begins to connect more deeply with friends, your role is to become more of a coach or advisor. You are on the sidelines, cheering them on, providing useful strategies, and helping them off the field when life knocks them down.

Making Friends

If your relationship with your child has been positive, respectful, and mutually engaging, the friends they attract will likely relate to them in a similar way. Their friends will be respectful and supportive because your child has grown to expect these qualities in a relationship. Alternatively, if their relationship with you has been one of submission to your authority or one in which they have little voice, you may find them attracted to friends who are more domineering. However, exceptions abound, so steer clear of judging yourself based on the people your child befriends. Some friendships form out of convenience. Examples include two children who find themselves in the same classroom and on the same sports team, neighbors who carpool together to school, or even students the teacher has paired up in group activities.

The people we spend our time with are important. Our friends, family members, and co-workers all influence us with their opinions, biases, beliefs, and insecurities. The same is true for your children. As you coach them, help them to see how others are influencing them. To step in and demand a child not see a friend because you don't like them or to push another person onto your child because you see potential is not coaching; it is directing. It is important for your child to make these choices, learn from the poor ones, and see how good ones play out. The more you allow them to live their own lives, the more likely they will find a direction and peer group that serves them well.

Close Friends

More than likely, your child will develop a best friend during this time. You will probably find yourself getting to know this child very well, along with their parents. Because children at this age are not yet independent, you will still be a part of their world and may find you will have a new group of friends yourself—the parents of your child's friends. Embrace this time and enjoy outings, events, school plays, and celebrations with these families. It shows your child that you value them and their friends.

When you support your child's friendships, your child learns trust and feels valued. Alternatively, you do not want to use their friendships as a means to manipulate their behavior. Threatening to keep them away from their friends to make them comply with a request only generates anger and resentment. As your child discovers you may use things they love to get the behavior you want, they will stop telling you about those things. They will no longer share stories about friends and may even pretend they don't have friends simply to keep you from taking away that which they most cherish. When your child feels they have to hide their true feelings, carry an "I don't care" attitude, and always be on alert to threats, their heart will close down. You want your child to live with an open heart. Therefore, it is important not to punish your child by keeping them away from their friends.

TIME MANAGEMENT

Some of the mistakes your preteen might make during these years are the result of being detached from the importance of time. They may lose track of time and come home late or procrastinate and end up staying up into the late hours of the night to finish a project or paper. You may find they can sleep until noon on any given Saturday. As with many of the other areas we have discussed, this lack of attention to time is not all bad. Our children are at a stage when they can become completely absorbed in an activity. You may have experienced this sensation when running, painting, or participating in some other activity. We lose all sense of ourselves and time as we experience what some call "flow." Our children have a natural tendency toward this positive experience. However, we recognize our children need to complete their homework, attend school, and come to the table when dinner is ready. Our sense of duty is often at odds with their sense of timelessness. Keep in mind their tendency toward being in the flow when you find yourself becoming frustrated with your preteen's lack of response to your requests. They really are not intentionally ignoring you; they simply have lost track of time. Let's look at some parenting strategies for preteens to help improve time management.

Provide Notice

One method to get your preteen's attention when you really need it is to give them some warning. "Wake" them out of their engagement with a ten-minute warning. "Dinner in ten!" is what you'll hear at our house. Providing early notice will give your children a few minutes to wrap up what they are doing or come to a good stopping point. To make an instant demand such as "Come to the table now!" is more challenging for them and will create a frustrating situation for everyone. It will be frustrating for you because they won't drop everything and come running, and it will be frustrating for them because they won't be able to drop everything quickly as their brains simply won't shift rapidly enough. Find a system you and your children can agree on—a dinner bell or a fun song—anything to get them out of their head and into the present moment, so they have some time to shift gears and join you at the table.

~~~~~~~~~~~~

**"...time management skills don't come naturally.
They are skills we learn over a lifetime..."**

~~~~~~~~~~~~

Natural Consequences

As you might imagine, when preteens find themselves absorbed in the moment, engaged with friends, or out on a bike ride, being late can become an issue. Late for school, late arriving home, late with their homework… You name it. Learning about time management is a challenge. It is interesting to me how we sometimes expect our young people to know this with little or no practice or experience. They should simply *know* they need to watch the clock, set a reminder, or gain the skills necessary to sense how much time has passed. However, time management skills don't come naturally. They are skills we learn over a lifetime of making mistakes and practicing. You need to support your child as they learn these skills without the additional pressure of threats and punishments. Turning in late homework is bad enough without also being grounded or having to listen to a tirade about laziness. Fortunately, the world provides plenty of feedback when we miss deadlines or find ourselves running late; parents do not need to add to it. This might be a time to caution parents on the "consequences" philosophies included in some parenting advice. Natural consequences are just that—natural. Imagine saying to a preteen, "If you don't get your homework done on time, there will be consequences—no phone next week." This outcome is not a consequence. It is a punishment in disguise, and this will be clear to your preteen. Taking away their phone is using your authority to bully them into getting their homework done. It's not such a great motivator. It may work in the short-term, but as we learned earlier in this book, it has lasting negative implications. Your child will hate doing their homework even more, and external demands will motivate their behavior rather than healthy internal motivation. A natural consequence in this situation is a lower grade, a conference with their teacher, or extra homework.

Plan Together

What are some ways you can support your child in learning to manage their time more efficiently? Each preteen may need different types of support. Stay cued into your child to see what motivates them in other areas of their life. Let's take the example of getting home on time. After an instance when they arrive home late, talk to them about how it made you feel, ask them what happened (remember they need to be heard, and their intentions were not bad because they're learning), and brainstorm what they might do next time to ensure they leave their friend's house on time to get home. You may need to simply point out that they need to plan for the time it takes to walk home. You may need to work out a plan for them to call you when they are running late. Perhaps your family can set up a buffer—everyone has a ten minute window, and if you're home at the agreed upon time, give or take ten minutes, all is well. Not punishing does not mean a lack of boundaries or rules in your home. Your children will learn to respect boundaries when they live within a supportive and respectful family unit. If you achieve compliance only through threats, it will only be temporary. If your child truly understands the importance of boundaries, and everyone in the family has a voice in setting those boundaries, cooperating will become second nature.

Completing household contributions or chores on time is another scenario. Taking the trash out has natural consequences—a smelly house. However, you may be more attuned to this consequence than your preteen. To encourage chores are completed in a timely manner, your best course of action is to set a routine and ensure everyone follows it. Getting into a pattern of completing chores supports everyone. At our house, we have many animals to feed. Once we finish dinner, everyone does their associated chore   dishes, feeding the dogs, feeding the goats and horses, and locking up the chickens for the night. In the case of taking out the trash, if all of the smaller trash cans around the house need to be emptied weekly, the person responsible finishes the chore before leaving the house on Saturday for weekend activities. If it is a daily routine, I may pull the bag out of the can, and my preteen takes it out before school.

Be Flexible

If your preteen forgets to take out the weekly trash or simply runs out of time on Saturday and needs to get to practice, you can address the situation in a couple of ways. "Hey, you forgot to take the trash out this morning, so I went ahead and did it for you. In exchange, can you help me unload the dishwasher this afternoon?" This strategy helps your child recognize they need to be responsible for taking out the trash and gives them the opportunity to make up for their oversight. If they resist helping with the dishwasher, ask them what other contributions they're willing to do in exchange; let it be their idea, and they will be much more likely to follow through. If it becomes a common oversight on their part, talk to them about it. "I see you missed taking out the trash on two of the last three Saturdays. Do we need to look at a different time? A different chore?" We're all in this together to keep the house in order and keeping pets and plants healthy. Work together to determine what contributions work best for the people in your family.

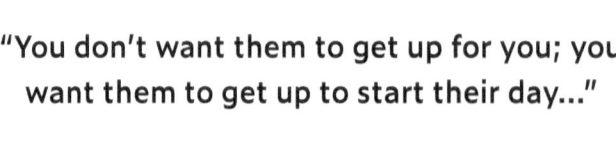

"You don't want them to get up for you; you want them to get up to start their day..."

Encourage Creativity

Another time-based struggle for some preteens is getting up on time. Morning after morning, they run down the stairs at the last minute, shoes in hand, backpack dragging, racing to the car or bus stop. These mornings are stressful for everyone. Your night owl might have been up until midnight engaged in a homework assignment or the latest online video. The 6:00 a.m. alarm comes too early, and they turn it off without even realizing it. Next thing they know, it's 6:50, and they have to be out the door at 7:00. They scramble to quickly brush their hair, grab a granola bar and water bottle, and race out the door. Attempting to make a change in the moment will be futile. Getting out the door is their single focus; stopping them at that point to discuss the situation will only create frustration. Find a time later in the day when everyone will be calm to discuss a better strategy. Perhaps it will be in the car on the way home from soccer practice. As we have discussed, their head will be in the game, so take a few minutes to shift their attention to the present. Ask about their day, how practice went, or about how their friend is doing. Then you can bring up the morning. "So, it seems like you had another rough morning—getting up late." State your observation and don't question them about what they did wrong. They will probably reply with some excuse or complaint about how early school starts. "I would like to help you think about some things you can do to make your mornings better. Have you thought about some changes you could make?" Take some time to brainstorm ideas based on what might work for this specific child. Remember, what works for you or their older sibling may or may not work for them. Perhaps setting an alarm for bed time or two alarms in the morning that are fifteen minutes apart would make it easier to get up. I had one daughter who struggled with the mornings until she found an effective solution—an alarm that would turn off only when you solved a math problem. The brain engagement helped her to get up. The important component is *she* found the solution, not me. She learned she can solve her own problems and find solutions that work for her. Had I purchased the app or found a different method, not only would it have been less effective, but also, I would have done the learning rather than her. Your goal is to position yourself as someone to help them learn how to make their mornings work for them, not be the compliance officer. You don't want them to get up for you; you want them to get up to start their day—for school, work, or an early morning sports practice—whatever lies before them.

Your preteen will sometimes need help getting motivated for what lies ahead in their day. If they have a challenging stretch at school, or perhaps are fighting with a friend, getting out of bed to start their day can be tough. Be compassionate and supportive and help them see how following through on going to school is important and will, in the end, help them move past these trying times. Challenging times serve us in providing accelerated growth and opportunities to learn. When we are in the middle of them, it is uncomfortable, but when we look back, we understand how these times formed and molded us into who we are today. Letting your child know how they handle and move through the challenges they experience in life will have a great impact on how they live now and as adults.

The next section will dive deeper into how to help your child learn to handle disappointment and life's other challenges.

LIFE CHALLENGES

When your preteen is going through an emotional time—and they will since their hormones will be in full swing—several strategies are available to support them. As a reminder, this is not a time for punishment, ridicule, or threats. They are already feeling down, perhaps unworthy or unsure of themselves; adding your negative input will create more hardship. Use your observation skills, and when you see your preteen withdraw or act differently, recognize this change as a sign they may be struggling. To ask, "What's wrong?" will often garner a shrug of the shoulders and a "nothing" in response. Share your observation. "It looks as though you are struggling with something. How can I help?" Again, you may get, "I don't know" in response but continue to offer ideas. You can share with them how it is often helpful to simply talk about a situation. The conversation doesn't have to lead to a solution, it is simply an opportunity to get things out in the open. If you can mention it, you can manage it (one of my favorite lines from the movie *A Beautiful Day in the Neighborhood*).

New Experiences

In some circumstances, your child may be looking for ideas on how to approach a certain situation, especially if it is a new experience for them. Always ensure your child is contributing ideas while you provide insight from your experience. This is not a lecture; it is a conversation. Both of you should be talking. You might ask your child what has worked for them in the past. Reflection is an excellent skill to instill in your child. Thinking back to past successes can provide the motivation and strength to move through challenging times. Let's look at an example. Perhaps your child is having an issue with a friend. They report Sean has always been a good friend, but Sean is getting jealous every time your child talks to their new classmate. Your child shares how they want to make the new person feel welcome, but they don't want to ruin their friendship with Sean. This is a common problem at this age as preteens learn how to be in relationship with others. It may be helpful to ask, "How do you think Sean is feeling?" Encouraging your child to consider other viewpoints is helpful and will provide ideas on how to handle the situation. What are some things your child could say to Sean, so they both feel better? Your child may also recognize that Sean may not be a good friend choice. You can help your child understand that friendships sometimes come to an end. Let them know they will have many friendships; some will be shorter, and some will last a lifetime. You never know how long someone will be a friend, so enjoy whatever time you have with them. When you know it's time to move on, acknowledge the end and remember the good times.

Disappointment

Another emotional challenge during the preteens years is the disappointment associated with not achieving a desired goal, not winning a competition, or not getting something they really wanted. We typically celebrate younger children for simply participating, but as children move into their preteen years, the disappointment of not landing on top is a much more common feeling.

The key to supporting your child through disappointment is to remind them of their individual differences and unique characteristics. Each of us brings unique strengths and gifts to life. The competitions in which we participate sometimes honor those strengths, and sometimes they don't. You want your child to recognize how the work we do is ours, and the activities we love are ours, and we do them because we enjoy them, not to win ribbons. Ribbons are fun to celebrate, but the real joy comes from participating, setting our own goals, and exceeding these benchmarks. This conversation may or may not take the sting out of losing, but it will plant an important seed for their future well-being.

Unfamiliar Emotions

A final challenge you may face as the parent of a preteen is your child's impending sexuality. During this age range, most girls will start their period, and both boys and girls will start to feel sexual attraction to others. Your preteen may have their first boyfriend or girlfriend during this time. These feelings are new and your preteen may be uncomfortable. Because of the newness, they will spend a lot of time talking and comparing with their friends, wanting to make sure they are normal and checking if everyone else is having a similar experience. Depending on you and your child, they may or may not feel comfortable talking to you about these feelings and experiences. This is the age when your child will blush if you raise the topic or if someone teases them about a boyfriend or girlfriend. Your role is to embrace and celebrate these changes. They mark a new developmental stage and signal that your child is growing and maturing into a healthy and capable adult, just as they should.

You may feel a desire to delay your preteen's development or protect their innocence. Be mindful of finding a middle ground that works for you and your family. Too much restriction will produce a power struggle. Your preteen will do everything they can to escape the restriction, including using deception. Maturation is not something you can stop. Alternatively, letting your preteen have free reign without any guidance might result in them feeling lost, confused, and unsupported. Work with them and have conversations, about what it means to be in a romantic relationship. How much time is appropriate? Where does this new relationship fit in with school, work, friends, and other activities? More than likely, the romantic experiences of preteens will be akin to puppy love. However, these relationships are the precursor to what comes next—teenagers.

CHAPTER 8:

TEENAGERS, AGES 15–19

THE TEENAGE YEARS ARE OFTEN the biggest struggle for parents. When your child is fifteen to nineteen years old, it can be challenging to realize the sweet baby you once cradled in your arms in the darkness of early morning hours is now driving themselves and arriving home at early morning hours. We replace the sleepless nights of getting up to feed a newborn with sleepless nights of worrying. Your child is going out into the world—high school events, work, college. It's hard. In this chapter, we'll explore how to support their sexuality, address the prejudice they may experience, confront substance abuse, and, finally, help your young adult manage separation. As you begin this chapter, take a minute to read "Guidelines for Parenting Teenagers."

GUIDELINES FOR PARENTING TEENAGERS

- The human brain is not fully developed until the age of 25.
- Compassion and generosity live in all of us.
- Spoken words carry emotion and have long-lasting impact.
- Each person has a gift and purpose.
- Service for others enriches life.

Our teenagers still need us, although they may not admit it. Their independence is exciting and terrifying all at the same time. You share in their joy, grief, frustrations, and celebrations. High school brings deeper relationships, pressure to figure out college and careers, and a preview of adulthood as teenagers experience newfound mobility, money management, their first car, and a job. Most of the heavy lifting of parenting has already been completed by this time. You have instilled the values and skills important to your family, and your child is now out in the world making more decisions and testing the landscape. Teenagers will now take their cues from friends and teachers. Your role is to be a haven should they fall and provide a listening ear should they need to talk to someone other than a friend. If you have parented with mutual respect and understanding, your teenager will now reciprocate with respect and understanding. Your days of creatively addressing misbehavior (rather than using punishment) have paid off. Your child is confident, thoughtful, and ready to make wise decisions as they set out on their own.

SEXUALITY

You probably have no qualms thinking about your own sex life. You have a child, so you have been sexually active at least once in your life. However, thinking about your child's sexuality can be challenging. It would be much easier if they could became nuns and priests. Developing sexual attraction is a normal stage in human development. You may have seen the early signs in your preteen, but as your child reaches their late teens, I can assure you they will find themselves experiencing sexual attraction. Some young people will be attracted to the opposite sex, and some will be attracted to the same sex. Regardless of their orientation, your role is to support them as they sift through all the online information, chatter from friends, and their own feelings.

"Each child will be different, and there is no one-size-fits-all solution when it comes to supporting your teenager in becoming a healthy sexual being."

I remember talking to a colleague about parenting. When the topic of sex came up, she said, "I know what I'm going to say. 'Have it!'" Her response was startling but certainly gave me food for thought. The comment made me realize all families and parents were unique, and an individual's approach to sexuality varies as much as hair color and temperament. As with most of the topics in this book, you need to think about what is right for your family and child. Each child will be different, and there is no one-size-fits-all solution when it comes to supporting your teenager in becoming a healthy sexual being. At no time is it more important to provide your young adult with ample opportunity to make their own decisions (and mistakes). Choices they make now have a more significant impact, but if you have allowed them a lot of opportunities to practice, they are good at it by now and will be able to apply what they have learned to these new experiences.

Communication

Not talking about sex with your teenager sends a negative message. If it is a topic you don't discuss, or if you become unreasonably uncomfortable, your child will assume sex is secretive or dirty.[26] It is normal to be a little uncomfortable; after all, intimacy between two people is private, and it is challenging to imagine your child as one of those two people. Remember, sexuality is a natural, normal, and healthy aspect of being human. Your teenager hears about it from friends, the media, and school, and they should also hear about it from you. For some parents, it is easier to start with conversations about dating. As with all your conversations up until now, ensure they are two-way. This is not the time to start lecturing. The same strategies that supported other topics also support human sexuality—open-ended questions remain truly questions and not "gotcha" questions, and observations ensure transparent communication. You might open the conversation with an observation. "It looks to me like you are attracted to Kelly." Your teenager may respond with a fact such as, "We are just friends," look embarrassed, or reply with something like, "Sort of." Next, you may be comfortable asking something like, "What does 'dating' mean to you?" Let your child share their opinion, chime in with what dating was like for you and compare the differences. Keep the conversation short and light. You want your teenager to feel comfortable talking about this part of their life.

A common myth claims that talking about sexuality may lead to your teenager engaging in sex earlier or more often. Research has shown the opposite to be true.[27] When teenagers engage with a caring adult, sexual development is a more positive experience, resulting in fewer unintended teenage pregnancies, longer waiting periods before sexual activity, fewer sexual partners, and increased condom use.[28] Make the time to talk about sexuality and share with your teenager how sexual development is an important and natural part of becoming an adult. The most common communication comes between mothers and daughters; however, it is important for both parents to have healthy conversations with their children, regardless of gender. The more open the conversation around sexuality and its important role in our lives is, the better. Their relationships now set the stage for future adult relationships, and it is important not to trivialize them. While dating as a teenager, your child will learn how to address strong emotions, communicate with someone they are dating, and negotiate their desires and boundaries.

Your teenager may resist conversations with you about their budding sexuality. Teenagers will more often reach out to peers, teachers, or other adults. Make sure your voice is heard as well and encourage your teenager to talk to other trusted adults. I have always supported my children connecting with the parents of friends, teachers, coaches, etc., so they feel they have a village of support. Sometimes another family member can be helpful. An aunt or older sibling or cousin can help your teenager better understand the world of dating and intimacy. Research in brain development called teenage sexuality the "elephant in the room."[29] Your child's interest in romantic relationships is right in front of you, but because it can be uncomfortable to discuss sexuality, you might dodge the opportunity to open communication. With many new experiences, you can do what educators call "scaffolding," a concept in which a teacher or parent provides significant support early on, and then gradually pulls away as the learner advances. When you recognize the early signs of sexual development, spend a little more time communicating about what it means to be in a romantic relationship, starting with the more mundane aspects. As your child develops, building confidence and understanding, you can begin to support them less and let them spread their wings.

~~~~~~~~~~~~~~~~~~~~~~~~~~~~

"Your teenager can go head-long into romantic adventures prepared with information, tools, and your support, or they can fall haphazardly in and out of relationships putting themselves and others in danger."

~~~~~~~~~~~~~~~~~~~~~~~~~~~~

Protection

If your family is like my colleague who had the "have it" response to questions about intimacy, you need to support your teenagers in practicing safe sex. If you are the family hoping your teenager becomes a priest or a nun, you still need to talk about safe sex. Research indicates that young people who are encouraged toward abstinence will still have sex but are much less likely to use condoms or contraception and thereby more likely to experience unwanted pregnancies.[30] Ensuring your teenager has access to protective "gear" for intimacy is similar to providing them with seatbelts and helmets, and it is just as important. Your teenager can go head-long into romantic adventures prepared with information, tools, and your support, or they can fall haphazardly in and out of relationships putting themselves and others in danger. Reproduction is the driving force behind humanity and the ongoing existence of our species. Your teenagers will be a part of this continuum.

Several approaches are available for talking to your teenager about appropriate contraception and protection against sexually transmitted diseases. To begin, research some of the current practices and recommendations. You may feel more comfortable reaching out to a family medical practitioner or someone within your religious community. The point is to make sure you discuss accurate and healthy practices with your child. Depending on your relationship with your child, the conversation could be light and funny, or it could also be more serious. Be consistent with your communication style as you embark on this conversation about staying safe during sexual activity. Making too much out of it will make it even more uncomfortable. Not talking about it at all is unsafe. Most often these conversations happen between mothers and daughters, but it is important to break this pattern and ensure mothers are talking to sons, and fathers are talking to daughters. By normalizing sexual behavior and establishing safe sexual practices, you will set your child up to have positive experiences as they venture into this new area of healthy human development.

Boundaries

Boundaries are important in all our relationships, but most certainly in our intimate relationships. Your teenager will learn all about boundaries through the many relationships they encounter during these years. They will learn how to tell friends they need time alone or some one-on-one time with a romantic partner. They will need to be able to tell someone how active they want to be in a sexual relationship, and they will need to be able to end a relationship when they realize it is not what they had expected. Learning to set boundaries is challenging and takes time. It also may involve making mistakes. Your role in supporting your teenager during this complex developmental time is to be available as a guide and confidante. If they reach out to you to share personal information, take it seriously and keep their confidence. If they come to you with questions, answer them honestly and respectfully. This is not the time for sarcasm, cynicism, or ridicule.

Miriam Arbeit, in her research on teenage sexual development, encourages families to take a positive approach to supporting teenagers.[31] She suggests rather than focusing on sexual activity as dangerous and risky, we should recognize how our young men and women are developing their sexual selfhood, learning about sexual negotiation, and evolving into sexually empowered individuals. Arbeit uses the phrase "sexual negotiation" to describe the process of setting boundaries. Establishing and maintaining sexual boundaries is a complex process involving personal beliefs and influences from family and peers. Remember, your teenager's friends are highly influential, so it is important to continue to talk with your child about their friends, what they believe, or how they might behave. Your role is changing. Your child is a short two or three years away from leaving the sanctity of your home; they need to make their own decisions now while they still have a safety net. Your role is to step back and watch. It's time to enjoy the wonder of witnessing someone go out into the world and explore new territories.

In the case of boundaries with intimate partners, it is helpful if your teenager sees you as someone they can talk to without fear of repercussion or punishment. If you have practiced a punishment-free approach to parenting, this will come naturally. If you have incorporated punishment throughout your child's upbringing, they will likely be less inclined to talk honestly with you. However, if you want to be their support structure, assure them you recognize it is time for them to take charge of themselves, and you won't punish them for mistakes. Many times, your teenager needs help accepting when it is time for a relationship to end. Whether they are on the receiving or giving end of a breakup, this is one of the most challenging components of an intimate relationship. Support them in maintaining a respectful approach (don't break up via text) and let them know we don't measure the quality of a relationship by its length, but by what we gain and learn from it. I can tell you from experience, when your child has a broken heart, it can also be heart-wrenching for you. Make sure you model a respectful response to the situation. We don't need to make the other person out to be the "bad guy." Good people end up in bad relationships. It doesn't mean those people are bad.

An important part of your conversation around sexuality and intimate relationships is the idea of consent. In any relationship, especially an intimate one, both individuals need to feel secure and respected. It is vitally important for you to reinforce "no means no" and silence also means "no." Only with a clear affirmation of "yes" from both individuals should young people move along with an intimate relationship. It is also important to discuss situations where alcohol, drugs, or even strong emotions may impede someone's judgment. If someone is not thinking clearly, their response will not be authentic, and their assumed consent is not valid. Sharing intimacy is a sacred activity, one to be honored and respected.

"...sexual health is inextricably bound to both physical and mental health."

Health

Here's a final word on sexuality. Health experts and those who study human development all agree that sexual health is inextricably bound to both physical and mental health.[32] Helping your child grow into a confident, empowered, and healthy sexual being is a gift. The foundation for healthy sexuality began early in this book when we discussed the importance of our children having agency—the ability to feel in control of their actions and what happens to them. Agency ensures they feel confident and able to carry out their ideas and plans. The parenting you did when your child was two years old will be evident in the teenager they become. The idea of agency can be expanded in this conversation on sexual health to ensure your teenager is aware of their own personal desires, they have a set of personal ethics and beliefs they can rely on, and they will continue to explore their own identity.[33] All of these skills—developed under your care—support them in having a positive adolescent experience. Your child's teenage years can be joyful and affirming when you have supported them, throughout childhood, to have a voice, make their own choices, and safely make mistakes, all without the threat of punishment.

PREJUDICE

You may find your child to be the victim of prejudice as they enter their teenage years. An underlying fear lives in many people—they see teenagers as thoughtless and sometimes even aggressive. Next time you are at the mall or another large public gathering, observe how infrequently people make eye contact with teenagers. It is significantly lower compared to the eye contact made with adults or young children. This unfounded ostracism can create a sense of insecurity in teenagers. They may not even be aware of why they feel isolated. Teenagers who identify as Black or Latino Americans face an even more threatening intersection of age and race as they walk the streets or through the mall. A study conducted several years ago by Hedin, Hannes, and Saito found that two-thirds of the teenagers they surveyed believed that the adults in their lives perceived them negatively.[34] Only a quarter of the teenagers believed that the adults in their lives held positive images of them. Additionally, most of the teenagers surveyed felt these negative perceptions were not accurate. Many young people live with this prejudice, creating an environment of mistrust and disrespect.

Explore Discrimination

It is important for parents to provide additional love and support during the teenage years. Your teenager may be pulling away and strangers may be looking away, but your role is to remind them of their value and the gifts they have for the world. The prejudice they experience comes in a variety of forms, from teachers who misunderstand their input to strangers who avoid eye contact. Continue to have talks about diversity and prejudice. Explain to your teenager that discrimination in the world is often unconscious. If you were to ask someone if they disliked teens, they would more than likely say no, though their actions may reflect otherwise. Each of us carries an entire lifetime of influence. We are influenced by societal norms, cultural standards, and family beliefs. The solution for us is to begin to see the individual, not the person's skin color, hair color, age, or speech patterns. It is to recognize that each person has a unique gift for the world.

Positivity

When you talk to your teenager about how people respond to them, remind them of the general good nature of humans. Remind them not to take prejudice or discrimination personally. The best way to counter discrimination is not to get angry, but to develop a relationship with the person in question. Once someone gets to know another person, they will only see the individual, not all the outer representations of race, age, and gender. In their book, *Survival of the Friendliest*, authors Hare and Woods share research on people who put their own lives at risk to help persecuted individuals.[35] They shared research on people who hid Jewish families during the Holocaust and those who supported the emancipation of slaves. The common link between all of the rescuers was they had all known an individual who, at some point, fell within the victimized group. It may have been a former school friend, neighbor, or colleague, but all of them knew a person who was Black, Jewish, or any number of other persecuted populations. If your child is feeling mistreated by a teacher, coach, or parent of a friend, help them find ways for the unfriendly adult to get to know them better. As the research indicates, it is more challenging to discriminate against someone when you actually know them as an individual. Encourage your child to stay after class and ask a question, then share a story about their life. Let the person know they have siblings, what kind of work their parents do, and the extracurricular activities that inspire them such as painting, horseback riding, or sports. Engaging with them is a better strategy than walking away and feeling the pain of prejudice.

~~~~~~~~~~~~~~~~

"...support is an important gift— independence with a safety net."

~~~~~~~~~~~~~~~~

One of the hardest aspects of being a parent is seeing your child struggle. Remember they are on their own path, and the struggles they encounter will support their development in the next stage of their journey. Be there to support, not fix. Your teenager is old enough to begin to resolve their own conflicts with school, friends, and others. Only when you see a dangerous situation too large or complex for them to handle, should you step in. Always ask if they want your help. When one of my teenagers struggled with a teacher, I would ask, "Would it be helpful for me to have a conversation with them too?" Typically, my children would say no, but they knew I had their back, and I was available if needed. This support is an important gift— independence with a safety net.

SUBSTANCE ABUSE

Teenagers are at a developmental stage when experimenting with all matter of "adult" activities comes into play, including alcohol, tobacco (in its many forms), and marijuana. Because these enticements are off limits, they will become more appealing. If ever there is a time you'll want to punish, it will be when you catch your teenager drinking or smoking. Because the consequences appear severe, you will want to react and stop the behavior immediately. You know punishment is an instant resolution, but remember it is not a long-term solution. You might stop the immediate behavior, but you won't be addressing the actual issue and will instead contribute to poor behavior later in life. To belittle them or to be authoritarian will only reinforce their motivation to use negative behavior to prove to you they are an adult.

Provide Information

The key to addressing this type of behavior, when your teenager is suggesting they are adult enough to handle alcohol or other illegal substances, is to actually treat them like an adult, not a child. If an adult friend was abusing a substance, would you punish them? No. You would talk to them and help them better understand the situation. Your role now as the parent of a teenager is to invite them into the circle of adulthood. Let's look at how you might handle underage drinking. You might find an empty can of beer on the floor of your teenager's car or smell alcohol on their breath. They may even slip and mention it in a conversation about a party. Once again, don't start with accusations. An emotional "Are you drinking?!?" will only cause them to panic and either lie or become defensive. Instead, start a calm conversation with your observation. "I found an empty beer can in the backseat of your car. It is pretty common for young adults to experiment with drinking. Tell me about your experience." Now you have opened the door to a conversation where your child will feel safer discussing the situation. You will have a calm teenager to talk with about how to drink responsibly, why age limit laws exist, etc.

Coach

When I was writing this book, vaping was a common activity for young people. Vaping is another form for taking in nicotine, and as with smoking cigarettes, it is addictive and harmful to a person's body. If your teenager is choosing to participate in vaping or any other harmful activity, there is no punishment strong enough or threat forceful enough to stop them. They will simply figure out more ingenious ways of hiding the truth from you. Your influence comes second to that of their peers. Your role is to serve as a coach and possibly a confidante. If you find vaping paraphernalia in your teenager's room, let them know and have a conversation. Even a quick text message can open the door. Snap a photo and remind them, "Hey, you know this harmful. Let's talk." If you take the time to have a conversation about tobacco and vaping, you will be assured your teenager is informed the next time a friend convinces them to experiment.

The most important aspect of how your teenager will navigate through these kinds of challenges is their experience with you over the last sixteen years. Do they feel supported? Do they feel trusted? Do they feel respected? If so, your child will be less likely to experiment, and if they do, it will likely be minimal. If the last sixteen years have created a sense of worthlessness, a need to prove maturity, or a feeling of anger at having been controlled, they will be more likely to experiment and at higher rates. From their perspective, what do they have to lose? Alternatively, if your teenager has a supportive and close connection with you—one they value—they will think twice before jeopardizing your trust. As always, if your child exhibits life threatening behaviors, it is imperative to seek professional help. Crisis hotlines are widely available, and the professionals associated with these organizations have tools to support your teenager or young adult in recovery.

SEPARATION

I have observed an interesting phenomenon when children approach a developmental stage in which they are destined to separate from you. These stages typically come around the age of seven, again at about fourteen, and when they embark on adulthood—heading off to college or into their first career. This phenomenon is a display of unhappiness with the relationship. As humans, it is easier to separate from someone if the relationship is painful rather than pleasant. The need to create a painful experience to have an excuse to leave is probably at its strongest during the teenage years. You will see glimpses of it at earlier stages (terrible twos), but because your child is now preparing to go out into the world on their own—a big step, to say the least—you will really see it during this phase.

Preparation

Preparing for this phase and living through it is not easy. It is a challenging time for a parent, especially if you tend to see yourself as your child's protector. You think of all you have done for them, all you have sacrificed, and this is what you get in return? It most certainly can be a challenging time. Throughout the years, the separation dance of needing you and loathing you will ebb and flow. They may snuggle up on the couch with you in the evening, and the next day, they may roll their eyes at everything you say. You may experience stretches during which they don't want to talk to you punctuated by long conversations about friends and school. Periods may arise when they seem to be gone all the time, spending time with friends and classmates. They are testing their independence, feeling the normal drive to go out into the world, and it is easier for them if they can create a rift with you. It is not unlike a couple seeking separation. Our culture expects something must go wrong, that one of the partners (or both) must be bad for a relationship to end, when, in fact, relationships between two good people sometimes do not work, and it is better for both people to go their separate ways. In your family, neither you nor your child is a bad person or at fault; it is simply time to let go. Your young and inexperienced teenager cannot see the situation as clearly as you. They may need to create tension (an excuse) to spend time away and to leave for college, the military, or a new job. It makes it easier for them, even though it may be painful for you.

Balance

Your challenge is to walk the fine line between being understanding and setting boundaries for respectful engagement. You do not want to make everyone in the house miserable because your teenager has created a hostile environment. Alternatively, you also want to create a space where your teenager can be true to themselves without threat of punishment or ostracism. Some days may go well, and others may not go so well. Be kind to yourself and your teenager, knowing the process of becoming an adult can be messy. Here's an example of what setting boundaries might look like. Your teenager has been sullen and argumentative for several weeks, and everyone in the house is walking on egg shells. You have been patient and kind and have let them have their time, but the unpleasant and unhealthy environment has gone on too long. If you angrily confront your teenager, they may feel caught off guard, having not even been aware of how their actions are affecting others. A confrontation will put them on the defensive or cause them to self-isolate even more. Instead, have a conversation. Begin with how you feel and outline your observations. "I have noticed lately you are spending more time in your room and not talking to us. When you talk to us, you come across as if you are irritated with us. It makes me feel uncomfortable and a bit disrespected. Can we talk about what you're feeling?" At this point, your teenager may open up, or they may not. Continue trying to open the door. You may even want to add something referencing their position. "I suspect you aren't even aware of how your behavior is affecting us." As you might recall, we are most likely to lash out when we are hurting. Work to separate your personal feelings from your parenting. It is not easy, and we all sometimes fall into self-defense responses with our children. Do your best during this time of separation and know the situation won't last forever. One day, they will call for advice on how to do laundry at college or how to manage a tough co-worker at work. If you have laid the foundation for a healthy relationship, a little teenage separation anxiety won't cause the house to fall.

Your child's teenage years will bring you some of your most fond memories and your most challenging moments. It is a time of exploration, when your child takes a giant step away from their family of origin and truly transitions from a child into a young adult. Treasure these years as you did their younger phases. Create a safe environment free from punishment and threats and be open to honest conversations and help them to feel safe to share successes and failures. Create a safety net for them to push themselves and try new pursuits. Let them spread their wings and test them out, but also let them regress when needed to the comfort of their room, the relief of a home-cooked meal, and shoulder to cry on. I imagine you will also grow during this timeframe. You will learn that letting go does not mean loss; it means your child is heading toward a new beginning and new adventures, with new meaning for your relationship. I have vivid memories of dropping my older children off at college and sharing in the excitement of their first apartment. I also have memories of picking them up when they needed support, holding them while they grieved, or talking them through a tough decision. I wouldn't trade any of it.

PART III:

IT BEGINS
WITH YOU

CONGRATULATIONS FOR MAKING IT THIS FAR. Parenting can be demanding, and as the previous section of this book illustrated, the challenges change as your children grow, mature, and become young adults. In these final two chapters, I share tips on how you can take care of *you*. Ensuring you take time to take care of your needs is critical. Ensuring you are happy, healthy, and fed will allow you to bring your best self to all of your relationships, most importantly to your relationship with your child. This section will cover physical, emotional, and finally, spiritual care. In the final chapter, I summarize my journey, sharing my personal discoveries and successes, some of the challenges I faced along the way, and encouragement as you embark on *your* journey. Enjoy.

CHAPTER 9:

PARENTS NEED LOVE TOO

THROUGHOUT THE PREVIOUS CHAPTERS I outlined the importance of being creative, how to recognize the unique needs of each of your children, and alternative practices you can use to create a punishment-free environment. As I review this material, though, I realize a key component of this practice is *you*. This chapter has to do with how you take care of yourself, maintain awareness of your own emotional responses, and step outside yourself to watch your own thoughts, words, and actions. Simply put, it's about self-awareness. Parenting is not for the faint of heart, and along with all the joy we anticipate when we first hear our child's heartbeat comes hard, yet rewarding, work. Some of the work is learning how to parent, and some of the work happens on the inside. To be your best you, take time to consider your physical, emotional, and spiritual needs.

PHYSICAL

My partner and I frequently reference the airline advice to put your own oxygen mask on first before helping your child with theirs. The underlying message is if you don't have enough oxygen, you won't be available to help anyone else. This idea is never truer than with parenting. We make every effort to make sure our toddlers aren't tired, hungry, and cranky, but do we stop to consider ourselves? I had an aha moment many years ago. My patience was stretched thin almost every day during the drive home after work with my children. There were two stops I had to make to pick them up from school and a caregiver, then I could head home. I realized that the five to six hours between lunch and my pick-up routine was simply too long; I was starving and cranky by the time I arrived home. I tried having a snack at work at around 4:00 p.m., and it completely changed my experience. I finally had the patience and calmness needed to get everyone picked up from their day and make it home for some family time. The car ride turned into a pleasant time to connect, rather than a time to merely endure.

~~~~~~~~~~~~

"It is so important for your own sanity—and for creating a positive environment for your children—to find ways to eat well..."

~~~~~~~~~~~~

Eating

Taking time for regular nutritious meals is important when managing your overall health and attitude. Most of us become short-tempered and "hangry" when we have gone too long without eating or have only eaten sugar and fat. It is important to energize our bodies and minds with a wide range of foods. Raising children is time-consuming, and it is easy to fall into bad eating habits. Find ways to ensure that quick, healthy snacks are available not only for your children, but also for you. Keep carrot sticks, cheese slices, whole grain crackers, and fruit within easy reach during the day. We have already talked about the challenges of morning routines, but you can eat a hard-boiled egg for some protein to start the day. Another common option is a protein shake or fruit smoothie to start off strong. Find what works for you. It is so important for your own sanity—and for creating a positive environment for your children—to find ways to eat well and keep your energy high and your body healthy.

Additionally, find ways to eat dinner at home as many nights as possible. Eating out adds unhealthy calories, salts, and fats. I know when you have soccer, dance, theater class, or other various evening activities, it is easy to use the drive-through as a dinner plan. Fast food is okay every now and then, as long as it doesn't become the norm. Sharing fresh, home-cooked foods and cooking together in the kitchen provides for a healthier lifestyle, and the healthier you are, the more you will have to offer your children. Many of the stories from this book have come from our dinner table. It is the one time you will have together as a family, especially as your children reach adolescence. It is an opportunity to catch up on everyone's day, share funny stories, solve problems, and connect. Cooking and cleaning are also times to connect. Rather than viewing these activities as unavoidable chores, see them as an integral part of your day, as well as time to reinvest in your family.

Sleeping

Need I say more? For parents of infants, sleep becomes a sought after luxury with very few opportunities for long stretches. During those early years, do what you can to get as much sleep as possible. Nap when your baby naps, and find friends to come over for a few hours to take care of your baby, so you can get some sleep. If you have a partner, trade off nights, so each of you gets a good night's sleep at least once a week. There is no magical solution to address sleep loss, especially if you have a baby who doesn't sleep well, but those days will end. Once your child can sleep through the night and no longer be the reason for your wakefulness, you may still find it challenging to sleep. Getting enough sleep is important to your quality of life. I highly recommend that you focus on maintaining a healthy sleep cycle. When you feel rested, you will have the energy you need to be supportive, patient, and creative with your children. If you are tired, as with when you're hungry, you will find yourself short on all these attributes. You will be impatient, angry, and quick to make threats and use punishment to influence your child's behavior. To enhance your ability to sleep soundly each night, here are some ideas:

- Go to bed and get up at the same time each day.
- Stop eating and drinking two hours before bed.
- If you wake up in the middle of the night and can't get back to sleep, get up and do something else. You want to associate your bed with sleep, not feelings of worry.
- Get plenty of exercise during the day.
- Initiate a regular bedtime ritual.
- Keep a journal next to your bed to write down to-dos and ideas that come to you, so you can return to sleep.
- Avoid caffeine in the afternoon and evening.
- Stay away from screens (phones, computers, etc.) an hour before bed.

If these ideas don't work, reach out to a medical practitioner for support. Getting a good night of sleep will not only sustain you in your role as a parent, but it will also support overall health and enhancement of all your relationships.

Exercise

In addition to eating well and sleeping well, exercise is an important tool for maintaining your physical body. As with so many things in our lives, how we exercise is as unique as our smile. There are many ways (none of them right or wrong) to ensure your body has opportunities to move and stay strong. Exercise is also a great mood lifter, so even a few minutes a day is beneficial for mothers of young children. It can be hard to prioritize exercise when you're caring for a family. Chores are almost always needing to be done—laundry, cooking, cleaning, yardwork—so this recommendation probably takes the most discipline. Remember the oxygen mask and remind yourself how taking a few minutes to exercise will actually give you more energy and a better attitude for all those tasks on your to-do list, and it will also support your ability to be patient and creative with your children.

You need to determine what works for you based on what you enjoy and what time you have available. Your exercise routine will also change throughout your life. We all have a friend (or maybe it's you) who runs marathons and is inspired to run every day. We also have friends who do very little, and we have friends who fall in between these two extremes. You need to decide what's best for you. Research suggests the four most important types of exercise are aerobic exercise, strength training, stretching, and balance exercises.[36] Work a variety of exercises into your life. I spend ten minutes each morning doing a stretch and balance routine. At least two or three times a week, I go for a 30- to 45-minute walk. In the past, I have played racquetball, and also did yoga for several years with one of my daughters. You will find that your exercise routine evolves and changes as you do. The key is finding some time to invest in your body with physical activity.

～～～～～～

"Regular physical exercise enhances
cognition, reduces depression and
anxiety, and improves sleep."

～～～～～～

Experts associate many physical benefits with regular exercise, including weight management, stronger bones and muscles, and increased life span.[37] However, the benefits that are most important to you as a parent are the mental and emotional ones. Regular physical exercise enhances cognition, reduces depression and anxiety, and improves sleep. In fact, research from the Center for Disease Control (CDC) shows adults who exercise regularly have increased sleep efficiency, quality, and depth. Additionally, they have reduced daytime sleepiness and require medicated sleep aids less frequently. Getting regular exercise is like getting a two-for-one. Not only do you support the well-being of your physical body, but you also contribute to the previous area of self-care—sleep![38]

As you step in and out of different exercise routines, it is important not to chastise yourself for missing a day here or there. Your exercise regimen needs to work for you, not anyone else. It needs to keep your body moving, address your unique body type, and provide some enjoyment. Whether it is riding a bike, lifting weights, doing yoga, or simply walking, make it your own.

EMOTIONAL

Next, you need to consider your emotional needs. Your emotions trigger your actions, and as we strive to provide a punishment-free home environment, considering our own emotions is paramount.

Relationships

An important component of caring for yourself is to make sure you support the relationships outside of your parent-child relationship. It is easy for a parent to step into the role of a mom or dad who is always there. When you care so deeply about your child, it is hard to imagine that anyone else can care for them like you. However, you need to let others care for your child so you have time for your own emotional needs. On a side note, having other adults in your child's life is critical to their development. Feeling loved and supported by a community goes a long way toward developing into a healthy adult. Your child should see grandparents, aunts, uncles, neighbors, and your friends as supportive adults in their life. In addition to creating community for your child, having other adults available to care for your child allows you to spend time with the people in your life whose relationships you value. If you are in a committed romantic relationship, it will need continued nurturing. On a regular basis, spend time together. Whether it is a weekly date night or a monthly weekend away, be sure to connect.

Maintaining a healthy sex life is also beneficial to your role as a parent and your intimate relationship. Intimacy is vital to a healthy partnership, and though you may feel exhausted from parenting infants or young children, connecting physically with your partner will increase your energy and well-being. The time you have for each other will ebb and flow. When your children are sleeping well and feeling well, it will be easier to find time for each other. When a child is ill, teething, or going through a rough time, it might be more challenging. Do the best you can, remembering that a healthy sex life contributes to health overall.

Making time for friends is another way to keep yourself mentally and emotionally fulfilled. You need adult conversations without the interference of young children. Getting together to laugh and share stories, talk about current events, or reminisce will keep you whole. You will be a much more available parent if you are whole. Of course, your relationships with friends will change as your family changes. When you have a brand-new infant, there is little time for anything else beyond caring for that little human. As your baby becomes a toddler, you will begin to re-establish closer relationships with family and friends. Your circle of support will morph, expanding and contracting as your family changes and grows. Be kind to yourself, give yourself permission to have adult time, and watch how your engagement with your child improves when you feel supported and loved.

〜〜〜〜〜〜〜〜〜

"If you are struggling emotionally, it is important to reach out to other adults, not your children."

〜〜〜〜〜〜〜〜〜

Each of us needs companionship and appreciation. Ensure you get these needs filled by the other adults in your life. A trap some parents fall into is expecting their emotional needs to be met by their children. A parent-child relationship is not a two-way street. You are in a position to nurture them, support them in healthy development, and raise them to adulthood. Your child is not here to do the same for you. This trap may play out in a few different ways. Sometimes it starts even before birth. A couple is struggling. Neither partner's emotional needs are being met, so they think having a baby will bring them together. They anticipate the love that's missing from their relationship will be available from the baby. With what you now know about parenting, you can see this is not a solution. Having a child will only exacerbate an unhealthy situation. This dynamic can also play out as one parent conspiring with a child against another parent. It may be a mother and daughter who gang up on a dad—spending time together shopping or crafting and leaving him to fend for himself. It could also be a father and son with secrets. "Don't tell Mom," does not support a healthy family life. As children grow into teenagers, parents may assume their young adults can be confidants or therapists. Neither of these scenarios is healthy for children. Childhood needs to be a time for learning, growing, and exploring, not for supporting adults. If you are struggling emotionally, it is important to reach out to other adults, not your children. If you still feel as though something is missing, or if you have significant feelings of depression or anxiety, seek professional assistance. We are not meant to go through this life alone. Humans are social creatures, and reaching out to ask for help is a strength. You will create a positive environment for both you and your child by ensuring you have supportive and loving relationships.

Interests

Our thoughts and emotions drive our behaviors, so being *aware* of our emotional selves is just as important as caring for them. To maintain emotional health, do the activities you love and the ones that bring you joy. Whether it is hiking, biking, cross-stitching, or baking, find time for these activities. You will have less time than you did before you became a parent, but look for small windows. Maybe let the dishes wait while you play a game of chess with your partner. Perhaps you enjoy writing—wake up thirty minutes early one day a week (or more) and work on a book of poetry. Whatever lights your fire, be sure to keep it in your life. Similarly, continue to learn. Take a class on Italian cooking, read a book on gardening, or learn to knit. Keeping your brain active will support your overall well-being and give you the energy you need to support the development of your child. You are modeling how important it is to continue growing and learning at all ages. Sit with your older child and read a book while they work on homework. Engage in thoughtful conversation at the dinner table, talking about something new that each of you learned over the last week. It should be easy to keep the spark of learning alive.

At some point, you may even be ready to go back to school yourself, whether it's to finish the bachelor's degree you started, get a graduate degree to advance in your field, or simply feed a desire for learning. Carving out time to learn becomes a must when projects or assignments are due. There are now so many opportunities to support working adults going back to school. You can find online programs, hybrid programs (part online and part in-person), and courses as short as five weeks. Look for solutions aligned with your needs and find programs with your lifestyle and interests in mind. College is not for everyone, but if you enjoy learning, it is a great way to stay engaged with life, while also supporting the growth and well-being of your children.

Regardless of your choices or interests, it is not selfish to find ways to do the activities you love and follow your curiosity. Investing in *you* gives you energy and strength to be the creative and patient parent your child needs. If your tank is drained, and you have no energy, your first instinct will be to find quick solutions to problems, which will often lead to threats and punishments. You and your child are in this for the long-term. You are working to create an adult who is confident, resourceful, and enjoys life. Take time to listen, be understanding, and bring compassion to your relationships. These tools will be in greater supply when you take care of yourself.

Triggers

Focusing on activities that support positive emotions is the easy part. We also need to explore the negative emotions stirring within us. This section explores what some refer to as "hot buttons" or "triggers." Hot buttons are those topics or actions, usually exhibited in others, which push you into an uncomfortable emotional state. The challenge with hot buttons, is they usually reside under the surface. We may not even know they exist. All we know is one minute we are feeling fine, the next we are highly agitated—maybe even angry—and ready to lash out. Strong emotions typically come on quickly and without warning. The slightest comment or action can push these buttons. Because of this, the offender is often confused and bewildered. How could my off-hand comment or action cause such a strong reaction?

Hot buttons and emotional triggers are the result of unresolved needs or traumas within our lives. Because of past events and experiences, we carry a sense of loss or feel we are missing elements of a happy life. When someone does something or says something to remind us of this missing part of ourselves, we react by lashing out to protect ourselves from further hurt or pain.[39] Usually, we are totally unaware of what causes the response. You may have long forgotten the experience which created the hot button, yet you still respond when triggered. Perhaps our own parents said something to us, causing us to fear abandonment. Our need to be liked or accepted will then be elevated to cover for the pain of feeling abandoned. In an off-hand remark, a child may be frustrated and say, "I wish I had a different family." If you did not have this hot button, you would recognize this comment as a need for comfort or a way of asking to talk about a bothersome topic. Alternatively, your emotional trigger of wanting to be liked and loved (not abandoned) could be triggered. Instead of seeing the comment as insignificant, you may take it to heart and respond more intensely than needed. You may lash out with a comment such as, "Fine! Go find another family," or you might withdraw from your child and tell them how their comment made you feel sad.

Neither of the previously described responses are rational, but they feel as though they come out of nowhere and are hard to stop. Your feelings come from within you; a child doesn't make you feel a certain way. You process their actions through your healthy perspective or through your wounds. If you maintain your own healthy perspective, you will be available to support them and understand why they are feeling hurt. Why do they wish they had a different family? What are they experiencing to cause such a response? Alternatively, your buttons and your negative response will only make these situations worse. The two of you will then be embroiled in a downward spiral. You will continue to feel the pain from your past and lash out with blame, so you will not be able to address the pain your child expressed in the first place. You will also likely want to punish—send them to their room, take away a beloved activity, or verbally scold them—setting into motion even more negative consequences.

Each of us has a trigger or two. Often, we have experiences or cultural exposure to ideas which suggest something is lacking in our lives. Examples of unmet needs include being autonomous, free, included, accepted, or right.[40] Your child's words or actions can inadvertently trigger one of these and before you know it, you will spiral into a sea of emotions. As you read this list, you may wonder how some of them could trigger someone while others may speak to you. Hot buttons are unique; what brings one parent to their knees will go unnoticed by another parent. Because of this variability, hot buttons are challenging for children to understand. A comment one parent finds acceptable may send the other parent into turmoil. This unpredictability is not healthy, so it is worthwhile to consider what your triggers might be and come to some resolution to better support creative and patient parenting.

Identification

To begin conquering your hot buttons, your first step is to identify them. Begin to notice times when you have a strong reaction to someone's comment or actions. Our bodies often react first. You may feel certain muscles tighten, your breathing may increase, or your heart rate may rise. Strong emotions will follow these body changes. You may feel frustrated, angry, or sad, and will almost always want to lash out. This physical and emotional response is meant to make the pain go away. Curiously, we are rarely aware of this process until it has already happened. This "unawareness" is what makes it so challenging to identify our hot buttons. However, a great start is to simply acknowledge we all have them. You need to start observing yourself. The next time you find yourself reacting strongly to your child, ask yourself:

- What were we talking about?
- What led me to respond this way?
- Is this response helping or hurting this relationship?
- Is it helping me to grow as a parent?
- Is it helping my child to make better choices?

By stopping to consider how your reactions affect the situation, you will be on your way to identifying your hot buttons. Once you have had time to consider these questions, you may want to spend some time thinking about what need they represent for you. Do you have an urge to be the authority? In this case, your child questioning your request to take out the trash might make you want to punish them by demanding that they have to take out the trash every week, rather than simply reinforcing the need for everyone to contribute around the house. Do you have a need to always be in control? When your child suggests a change in plans or expresses a conflicting desire, do you feel upset and disrespected? This hot button might send you inward, causing you to punish your child by withdrawing. Alternatively, a parent without this hot button may simply consider the alternative and have a conversation about the pros and cons of the different activities.

COMMON TRIGGERS

- Being questioned
- Feeling undervalued
- Needing control
- Feeling invisible
- Feeling used
- Experiencing vulnerability

One of my hot buttons is not feeling valued. When a family member casually disregards my question or doesn't respond positively to a suggestion I make, I feel undervalued and unappreciated. The comment may have nothing to do with how much my family member values me, but I take it to heart and begin to feel unwanted, undervalued, and angry that the comment and person made me feel bad. The key to recognizing hot buttons is those last few words I just shared, "They made me feel [bad, angry, frustrated]." In identifying our triggers and hot buttons, we need to remember that our feelings belong to us, and it is our thoughts, experiences, histories, and prejudices which make us feel the way we do. It may sound unbelievable at first, but others do not make us feel; we make ourselves feel. Our emotions are our own and any external experience may trigger us, but we are ultimately responsible. My children and partner have been caught off guard by my outbursts to what they considered offhand remarks. They may have been having a bad day, or were distracted by other thoughts and had no intention of causing me pain. When these emotions arise, a healthier response would be to share my feelings rather than lashing out. If your child responds with a grunt to, "How was your day?" you could let them know you feel undervalued by saying, "Hey, I feel as though you don't care when you don't even take a few minutes to respond to my question." They would probably be surprised by the response, and a conversation could ensue to encourage more understanding, rather than yelling and fuming about being underappreciated. Another solution would be to recognize this is just one of your hot buttons and let it go—assume your child values you and is simply too distracted with thoughts of schoolwork, friends, etc.

Shift Your Response

Once you have identified one or two of your hot buttons, think of some ways to support a healthier response. In the heat of the moment, you may not be able to stop the train, especially when you first recognize that your response may be out of alignment with the situation. Once the episode is over, spend some time contemplating what happened. Begin to think about how you might respond in the future. If you could replay the situation, what could you do differently? Depending on the case and the age of your child, you also may want to share with them. The conversation may take the form of an apology. "I want to let you know I can see how I overreacted earlier today. I read more into the situation than was truly there, and I am sorry I took it out on you." Not only does this response support your effort to change your behavior, but you will also be modeling a great skill for your child—how to accept responsibility for your actions.

"Find at least one other person with whom you can be yourself, share your concerns, and express your emotions."

It is not easy to learn to identify your hot buttons and change your behavior when something triggers you. This is the time to lean on your support network, partner, or adult friends. Talk to your friends and family to get their perspectives. Find ways to laugh and smile about how complicated life can be and recognize each of us has wrinkles and imperfections. If your feelings are overwhelming, let yourself cry and feel sorrow; your friends can offer a supportive shoulder or words of wisdom. The point is to not do this alone. Find at least one other person with whom you can be yourself, share your concerns, and express your emotions. In our world of social media, where most posts celebrate good times, we sometimes forget everyone has bad days and makes mistakes.

Another strategy to move past your hot buttons is to develop your inner voice.[41] It can help you navigate the waters of your own needs. Also referred to as self-talk, it is wise to keep this conversation positive as much as possible. However, you may also want to consider how the voice in your head supports your negative response to a situation. Considering my example, when you feel your emotions begin to rise, you can say to yourself, "Here it is again. I may not be able stop getting angry, but I can at least see I am consistent in getting angry when someone makes me feel undervalued." The next time, your inner voice may cause you to pause. "Here it comes. Can you do something different?" You will then be able to redirect your anger and express your feelings, rather than lashing out. With an older child, you can share how even though their lack of interest in sharing their day may mean nothing to them, it makes you feel disconnected or even unimportant. Finally, you might get to the point where your inner voice has transformed your hot button. After a comment which previously may have set you off, you might say to yourself, "Look at you. In the past, you would have felt angry; now you see it for what it is, and it is so much better not to waste your energy getting angry over it."

You can also approach the situation with curiosity. Be aware of when your body starts to respond, your muscles tighten, your heart rate increases, and your breathing becomes heavier. When you feel these changes in your body, say to yourself, "This is curious. Why am I getting so worked up?" Then, purposely try to change how you respond; consciously relax your muscles and slow down your breath. Bring yourself back to where you were before the comment.[42] You will have an improved perspective and will be able to approach the situation from a place of calm and reasoning. You will feel empowered by identifying the issue rather than feeling as though you are a victim of the situation.

Incorporate CBT

Another method to support your inner work is Cognitive Behavioral Therapy or CBT. Self-talk is also at the core of CBT. The Oxford dictionary definition for CBT is "a type of psychotherapy in which negative patterns of thought about the self and the world are challenged in order to alter unwanted behavior patterns or treat mood disorders such as depression." This definition indicates the breadth of this technique. You can use CBT to address anxiety and addiction, cope with grief or loss, manage stress, and resolve conflict.[43] When I wanted to lose weight, I incorporated CBT to change my thinking (and self-talk) around food and eating. For example, I simply shifted my thoughts when I first felt hunger from, *I need food to satisfy this craving,* to, *It's okay to be hungry.* Another example was to change my belief around throwing food away. I changed my self-talk from, *Children are starving in other parts of the world,* to, *It's okay to throw food away or add it to the compost bucket.* This example demonstrates how changing our words can shift our beliefs and actions. The program worked for me and assisted me in meeting my goal weight.

In the last section about hot buttons, I hinted at this technique, but you might consider using it for a variety of parenting challenges. For example, you may feel it is imperative to have all the toys picked up in the family room before going to bed. Even when you are exhausted, the voice in your head might prompt you, *Good parents keep the house in order.* I once talked to a woman who claimed she took time each evening to put all puzzle pieces back into each puzzle before putting them away, all while under the incredulous gaze of her husband. Consider changing these types of thoughts to bring more balance to your life. An alternative may sound something like, *Good parents provide a safe environment, even if it is sometimes messy,* or perhaps, *Picking up the house once a week will keep it in good order.* Shifting your perspective will allow you to release the stress and resistance inherent in self-talk. The woman who shared this story also shared how she found a way to relax and compromise on her need to be in control and keep everything in strict order. The change made a big difference in her life (and her relationship).

> "Your thoughts are a powerful
> influence on your emotions."

Research on parenting and CBT suggests the thoughts we have about our children's intentions can affect how we respond to misbehavior.[44] Think about your young child having a meltdown in a store for any number of reasons. Researcher Sandra Azar and her colleagues interviewed parents and found those who had thoughts and beliefs associating their child's actions with negative intent were more likely to respond with unhealthy parenting strategies. Examples are thoughts such as, *He's doing this to embarrass me,* or, *She is just trying to manipulate me*, which will only lead to frustration and a desire to demonstrate dominance over the child. Conversely, parents who did not attach negative intent and approached the situation with neutral or positive assumptions handled the situation with calmness and demonstrated healthier interactions. Thoughts such as, *He is tired and hungry, so of course he is having a meltdown,* or, *She doesn't have the tools yet to manage the strong desire for candy, I need to support her in learning*, will keep a parent calm and rational, rather than immersed in an emotional battle.

Your thoughts are a powerful influence on your emotions. As with hot buttons or emotional triggers, taking time to observe the thoughts in your head (your internal voice) can significantly change how you engage with life and your children. Your perspective about any given situation is changeable. Next time you find yourself harboring negative feelings, take a moment to consider what led to those emotions. Could you be wrong in how you assumed the other person was thinking or feeling? If you come out in the morning to a flat tire, what goes through your mind? The tire is flat and will need to be fixed. You have a choice in your thoughts and the corresponding emotions. You could think to yourself, *Why do bad things always happen to me? I can't believe I have to change this tire. Nothing seems to be going right, and now I'm going to be late for work.* Alternatively, your thoughts might be more like, *Everyone gets flat tires; it looks like it's my day to take care of one. I know my boss will understand. I'll give them a call and get started.* In both cases, the unchangeable fact was a flat tire needed changing. The difference in the two scenarios was the inner voice. The tire doesn't make you feel upset; it's simply a tire. Your thoughts have the power to cause unpleasant (or pleasant) emotions.

Will you always find the right belief or thought? Of course not. Days will still come when you will be short on patience or calmness. You will find yourself hungry or tired, and you may even say something to your child that you regret. The goal is for the majority of our interactions to be positive and supportive. It's like your checking account. As long as we ensure enough positive interactions are coming in to cover any negatives, our balance will remain positive. Our background and experiences mold our personality—including our hot buttons. These triggers and quirks make us who we are and sometimes serve to protect us. If you have created a strong foundation in your relationships, they will withstand a few negatives.

SPIRITUAL

Your parenting journey opens the door for you to begin a journey of your own. The challenges of raising another human (or several humans), can stir up our own past, issues, dreams, and desires. The more aware you are of *you* the more available you will be to those around you. This section supports parents in considering what goes on inside of them, rather than outside. What inspires you, gets you up in the morning, keeps you awake at night, makes you smile, or brings you down? This is the soul's journey—the part of you that is greater than the nuts and bolts of living life. It is the essence living within you—how you connect to it, feel its power, and find ways to live in this world with less pain and more joy.

Some people call these attributes emotional intelligence or social skills. Another common term is "conscious"—an awareness of your thoughts, words, and actions. The path varies based on each person's intellect and religious or spiritual practices. Considering what matters to you is what is most important. Ensure you take time to investigate your inner workings—what makes you tick, what you value, what holds you back, what causes you to suffer, and what makes you joyful. What follows are some suggestions on how to begin or continue this journey. If you are reading this book, you have probably already started. Some of the ideas will resonate with you, and others will not. These practices don't make up a to-do list; they are simply ideas on how to begin living a fuller, more enriched life, supporting your spiritual journey as a parent. Your mental, emotional, physical, and spiritual health are instrumental in creating a healthy environment for your child.

Faith

For some people, believing a source of inspiration, compassion, and caring exists outside of themselves and other humans can support their peace of mind and help them find comfort in times of need. I refer to this as faith—faith in God, faith in an all-knowing universe, or faith in the divine. Whichever way a person names it, sees it, or chooses to engage with it, this faith provides support. For many, organized religion is an option. A community of people led by a magnanimous leader sharing a common belief system creates the perfect environment for many to support the spiritual nature of humans. Churches and other religious gatherings provide a host of support mechanisms. In addition to a community of like-minded individuals, church serves to support people in need, encourages a life of service, and simply provides a dose of inspiration to keep us going each week.

Mindfulness

For others, individual connection with the spiritual side of being human is a better path. Meditating on a daily or weekly basis, reading spiritual books, bringing together small groups to share ideas, and engaging in personal prayer are all ways to connect and center yourself apart from the day-to-day activities that keep you so busy. Meditation is an effective technique to find your center and connect with your best self. Meditation comes in a variety of forms, and you can practice in groups, with a coach, or alone. Books, recordings, videos, and instructional tapes on meditation are available in the thousands. To find what works for you, try a few, talk to friends, or simply find a quiet spot, close your eyes, thank your mind for being helpful, and ask it for a few minutes of silence. The calmness associated with meditation will remind you how all of the frenetic energy associated with parenting is certainly part of your life, but it does not have to be *all* of your life. Find time for some quiet. I introduced meditation as the first practice in this section because it works for me. I meditated each morning before working on this book, even if only for a few minutes. The practice connected me to a part of myself from which I can see the bigger picture and the greater good, and it helped me find the insight I needed to share my experience with you, the reader.

Another key feature of meditation is its connection to the breath. To be conscious of breath entering and exiting the body, slow your breathing. Breathing deeply contributes physiologically to a sense of calm. In people who practice meditation regularly, scientists have measured a change in brain waves, shifting from a higher frequency to a lower and more consistent frequency. The shift works to lift your spirits and alter your body chemistry for the better. Research conducted at Harvard Medical School shows physical changes to the brain during meditation and even evidence of lasting effects throughout the day.[45]

You can easily find books and guided meditation tapes in bookstores, online, and through local libraries. You may want to experiment with several different options until you find what works best for you. The advantage to meditation is its low cost—it doesn't require any equipment or tools. A soft chair, a quiet room, and a few minutes of time is all you need. This is a practice. Some days will go well and you will open your eyes feeling refreshed and rejuvenated. Other days, you may find it almost impossible to turn off the voice in your head with everything you need to do. It's okay—simply keep at it and look forward to those days when it goes well because they will come. So much of our life's activity can push us into fight-or-flight mode, feeling a sense of urgency and a need to meet deadlines. Meditation counters this physical response with one that calms the body and the mind. By taking a few minutes for yourself each day, you will experience your role of parent as calmer and more focused. You and your family will benefit.

Practicing yoga can also bring forth a sense of peace and a feeling of being centered. Although not specifically a religious doctrine, there are various methods which include both physical and mental practices designed to promote intellectual and spiritual growth. I recommend you do research and experiment to find which type works for you. Research certainly indicates the physical component has positive effects on health; there are also professional articles supporting yoga's ability to aid the development of self-awareness and personal growth.[46]

I've shared with you a handful of approaches for spiritual work. However, a myriad of options is available. You need to find what works for you. Talk to friends, browse through book stores —sometimes books find you—and work with professionals. Resources for counseling and psychotherapy are readily available, and these services will help you talk through your inner world and how it affects your outer world. Other strategies include the use of affirmations or imagery or even physical techniques such as tapping, breathing, and yoga. For some people, a walk on the beach or through a forest provides a connection to something greater. The idea is for you to begin the journey into your own soul—your inner world. Your inner work is important. Author Jan Frazier says it well. "Nobody and nothing can save you from the open-eyed tunneling into your interior. It's why your spiritual practice, your path, your teacher, can take you only so far. Nobody can go with you. But go you must."[47]

This chapter on loving yourself covers the importance of physical, emotional, and spiritual care. The challenges we face as parents often bring us to our knees and cause us to question our approaches. Hopefully, they will cause us to act and make changes. Many parents eventually realize their children are their teachers, not the other way around. Take some time to reflect on what your parenting has already taught you and what you still might have to learn. Be grateful and appreciative of what a wonderful experience it is to be a parent and support another human as they learn to effectively live on this planet and make a difference in the lives of others.

CHAPTER 10:

THE JOURNEY CONTINUES

WHEN I REFLECT ON MY "grand experiment," I realize I never did find my children running naked through a forest. Instead, I discovered a wonderful truth that parenting can be a graceful and lovely experience with another human being. What I thought would be a gift to my children turned out to be a gift to me. I didn't have to be concerned about who was the boss or force them to do what I thought needed to be done. I enjoyed twenty years (so far) of simply loving, supporting, and holding a light up to them, so they could see how truly amazing they are. Every child is amazing, and when given a loving and supportive family, they can blossom into healthy and loving adults. As you embark on—or continue—your parenting journey, I hope your family also reaps similar rewards.

Removing punishment from the equation can remove the resistance between a parent and a child, a resistance which creates barriers and endures across generations. Being authoritative and trying to control another human being's behavior is hard and tiring work. Maintaining power over and ensuring compliance can be exhausting. It is such a gift when you realize you can lay down all those punishment strategies, relax, and simply parent from the heart with love, calmness, and creativity. We can keep an open heart, we don't need anger or frustration to achieve any authority, and we can let our child be in charge and explore on their own what it means to be human—what to wear, what to eat (we may need to provide some guidance), and how to spend their time. It becomes a collaborative project. We work together to get them through childhood and into young adulthood. They have a voice, we have a voice, and we find compromises and win-win solutions. My punishment-free strategy allows us to see how amazingly creative children can be in coming up with solutions in areas that are sometimes challenging for adults. Too often, we rely on solutions from the past, ones we use time and time again.

Throughout this book, I mention creativity as an important component of punishment-free parenting. Much of what we learn throughout our lives is how to control others with rewards and threats. Punishment as discipline has been a staple of many environments, including our families. We must look for new ways to raise our children and come up with creative solutions to age-old problems. We must be creative and thoughtful in how we help a toddler or a teenager address the latest challenge in their lives. We must be compassionate in conversations with our children, remembering they are as powerful and worthy as any member of the family, simply with a bit more to learn. We must be patient when our instinct is to send a child to time-out or take away a valued possession as punishment. We must be aware of the long-term consequences, not our own short-term need to quickly address the situation.

"Fun and creativity, in combination with intelligence and knowledge, is a recipe for raising children into healthy and happy adults."

Being creative means using our strengths and intellect to come up with original ideas. We typically view creativity as the realm of the artist or musician, but it lives in all of us and is a tool we can use in all aspects of our lives. We creatively solve problems at work, in our homes, and in our families. Each of us can be creative and look at problems from new perspectives. We can think of an outrageous solution and use it as a jumping-off point for a realistic one (or sometimes even use the outrageous solution). We can bounce ideas off other people, get some of their creative juices flowing, and find an answer together. Sometimes, our creative solutions come from intuition or what some call a "eureka" moment. No discussion on creativity is complete without Albert Einstein's perspective. One of the most intelligent individuals of our time, he recognized the importance of creativity and imagination, and we attribute to him many quotes on the subject including, "Imagination is more important than knowledge. For knowledge is limited to all we know and understand, while imagination embraces the entire world, and all there ever will be to know and understand," and, "Creativity is intelligence having fun." Fun and creativity, in combination with intelligence and knowledge, is a recipe for raising children into healthy and happy adults.

Raising my younger two children in a punishment-free environment also came with challenges. For one, the rest of the world still considers punishment to be an effective tool for managing children's behavior. As my children participated in sports and youth organizations, punishment was certainly used to coerce and control their behavior. Additionally, most schools use punishment (and rewards) to motivate and incentivize good behavior. The Montessori schools used very little, if any. However, the public high schools my two younger children attended still incorporate the age-old stick-and-carrot (punishment and reward) model for controlling behavior.

We see examples from school settings every day. Administrators suspend or expel children and young adults from school on a daily basis. Ironically, school is probably the best place for struggling children. If we want children to feel they belong in school, kicking them out, even temporarily, sends the wrong message. When we punish people, they rarely feel remorse; rather, they more often feel resentment. In the 2017–2018 academic year, school administrators suspended (required to leave for a short term) over two million students, and just over 100,000 students were expelled. Males and students of color were disproportionately affected by this treatment.[48] My children did not get suspended or expelled, but the threat of this punishment hung over them and their classmates. I was able to create a punishment-free environment at home, but not out in the world.

You may be wondering how my children felt about their punishment-free childhood. I asked one of them what they thought the effect was of never having been put in time-out, grounded, or deprived of their phones. My daughter's thoughtful response was, "I didn't know anything different, so it is hard to say. I do know that because I am not afraid of what might happen, I feel like I can tell you anything. I don't have to lie or be sneaky." Her response warmed my heart. I know the fear of negative repercussions and am grateful these two children didn't have to live with the ache of this apprehension, at least while they were at home. From my perspective, I can tell you I never once found them running naked through the forest. They also didn't talk back or rule the house with demands and entitlement. They are both well-adjusted and healthy individuals. They did well in school, made friends, and are approaching college with high hopes and dreams. They also experienced challenging friendships, disagreements with each other and me, and anxiety before tests and performances. I think the best is yet to come. I can't wait to see what kind of relationships they have and who they choose to spend their lives with. I will be interested to see how they raise their children, should they choose to have them. The work of creating a punishment-free home is not about the short-term benefits. It is about the big picture. How will they choose to engage with others at work? At play? How will they approach the challenges life throws at them? These are the life experiences I am most interested in affecting.

Two big world experiences prompted the writing of this book—school shootings and the 9/11 attacks. My goal was to change the trajectory of these wounded souls—those who see retaliation and punishment as the necessary tool to rectify a wrong, demonstrate commitment to their beliefs, or act on bias. I hope the teenager who is teased and ostracized will no longer feel the need to punish their classmates with violence. I also hope there are fewer classmates teasing each other. The devout believers who believe only one path is right will no longer feel the need, by flying planes into buildings, to punish those who don't believe or who live in direct opposition to their path. Individuals in positions of authority—those dedicated to serving and protecting our individual rights—will no longer dehumanize those who appear different, nor will they feel compelled to use unnecessary punishment.

Of course, I started small, with two unique souls born into my home. I don't know if sharing how to raise children without the use of punishment will shift the global paradigm, but I have to at least try. I'll end with one more quote from Einstein. "We cannot solve our problems with the same thinking we used when we created them." We need to change our mindset about the power dynamics within our homes, schools, relationships, workplaces, and communities. This change, and the associated end to punishment, is a new and different ways of thinking. It is the thinking we need to solve both large and small life problems. With new ways of relating, we can bring an end to the trauma that has negatively shaped our world and broken our hearts.

I hope you have found nuggets of information to support you in your parenting journey. It is most certainly the road less traveled and comes with pot holes, speed bumps, construction, and detours, but it also comes with beautiful scenery, new adventures, and stunning sunsets. I encourage you to keep learning and sharing your stories. I would love to hear from you about your parenting journey. You can contact me through my website at rebeccawoulfe.com.

ACKNOWLEDGMENTS

I AM GRATEFUL FOR EVERYONE who inspired me to take this journey and embark on my "grand experiment." First, I want to thank my children, Sarah, Annie, Madigan, and Maura. Without them this book would not exist. To my husband and life partner, Bill, thank you for your encouragement and support and for being patient with my early mornings and late nights. I couldn't have done this without you. To my parents, you inspired in me a passion for life and for making a difference. To Sandra, thank you for being such a great friend and champion of my work. Your generosity and wisdom have made a huge impact on my life.

To my editors, thank you for challenging me, improving my writing, and always reminding me to keep my readers at the heart of my message. To Kiki from KLR Literary Management, your ongoing support, positive attitude, and professional expertise have been invaluable.

Finally, a deep bow of gratitude to my teachers, Kathryn Kvols of the International Children's Network; Maria Montessori, founder of the Montessori approach to education; and Alfie Kohn, who first challenged me to consider the role of rewards and punishment in raising children. These leaders paved my way and sparked my inspiration.

ABOUT THE AUTHOR

REBECCA WOULFE, PHD, is a parenting mentor, educator, and mother. Her greatest joy is spending time with her family, friends, and her beloved animals—three dogs, two cats, two goats, two horses, and a half dozen chickens. She supports parents through mentoring and workshops in navigating their parenting jour-  neys using punishment-free practices, and serves as an administrator for a local community college. However, her most important work was raising her own children without punishment. Her extensive personal experience contributes to her ability to guide others on their parenting journeys. Rebecca was a certified parenting educator for the *Redirecting Children's Behavior Program* and has conducted extensive research on how punishment impacts children's behavior. She lives with her husband in the foothills west of Denver, Colorado where they enjoy spending time in the outdoors hiking and fishing. She invites readers to share their parenting stories and challenges. You can contact her through her website at rebeccawoulfe.com.

ENDNOTES

1 Kvols, K. (1998). *Redirecting children's behavior*. Chicago, IL: Parenting Press.

2 Straus, M. A. (2000). Corporal punishment by parents: The cradle of violence in the family and society. *Virginia Journal of Social Policy & the Law, 8*(1), 7-60.

3 Haney, C. (1998). Riding the punishment wave: On the origins of our devolving standards of decency. *Hastings Women's Law Journal, 9*(1), 27-78.

4 Straus, M. A. (2000). Corporal punishment by parents: The cradle of violence in the family and society. *Virginia Journal of Social Policy & the Law, 8*(1), 7-60.

5 Straus, M. A. (2000). Corporal punishment by parents: The cradle of violence in the family and society. *Virginia Journal of Social Policy & the Law, 8*(1), 7-60.

6 Gómez-Ortiz, O., Romera, E. M., & Ortega-Ruiz, R. (2016). Parenting styles and bullying. The mediating role of parental psychological aggression and physical punishment. *Child Abuse & Neglect, 51*, 132-143.

7 White, R. M. B., Roosa, M. W., Weaver, S.R., & Nair, R. L. (2009). Cultural and contextual influences on parenting in Mexican American families. *Journal of Marriage and Family, 71*, 61-79.

8   Bornstein, M. H. (2012). Cultural approaches to parenting. *Parenting, 12*(2-3), 212-221.

9   Straus, M. A. (2000). Corporal punishment by parents: The cradle of violence in the family and society. *Virginia Journal of Social Policy & the Law, 8*(1), 7-60.

10 Kohn, A. (1993). *Punished by rewards: The trouble with gold stars, incentive plans, A's, praise, and other bribes.* New York: Houghton Mifflin.

11 Kohn, A. (1993). *Punished by rewards: The trouble with gold stars, incentive plans, A's, praise, and other bribes.* New York: Houghton Mifflin.

12 Straus, M. A. (2000). Corporal punishment by parents: The cradle of violence in the family and society. *Virginia Journal of Social Policy & the Law, 8*(1), 7-60.

13 Mendez, M., Durtschi, J., Stith, S. M., & Neppl, T. K. (2016). Corporal punishment and externalizing behaviors in toddlers: The moderating role of positive and harsh parenting. *Journal of Family Psychology, 30*(8), 887-895.

14 Straus, M. A. (2000). Corporal punishment by parents: The cradle of violence in the family and society. *Virginia Journal of Social Policy & the Law, 8*(1), 7-60.

15 Obama, M. (2018). *Becoming.* New York: Crown Publishing Group.

16 Bandura, A. (2006). Toward a psychology of human agency. *Perspectives on Psychological Science, 1*, 164-180.

17 Kvols, K. (1998). *Redirecting children's behavior.* Chicago, IL: Parenting Press.

18 Brauer, J. R., & De Coster, S. (2015). Social relationships and delinquency: Revisitng parent and peer influence during adolescence. *Youth and Society, 47*(3), 374-394.

19 McKenna, J. J., & McDade, T. (2005). Why babies should never sleep alone: A review of the co-sleeping controversy in relation to SIDS, bedsharing and breast feeding. *Paediatric Respiratory Reviews, 6*, 134-152.

20 Kvols, K. (1998). *Redirecting children's behavior.* Chicago, IL: Parenting Press.

21 Academy of Nutrition and Dietetics Position Statement. (2013). Total diet approach to healthy eating. *Journal of the Academy of Nutrition and Dietetics, 113*, 307-317.

22 10 reasons not to hit your child. (2020). Ask Dr Sears. Retrieved from http://askdrsears.com/topics/parenting/discipline-behavior/spanking/10-reasons-not-hit-your-child

23 Montessori, M. (1966). *The secret of childhood.* New York: Ballantine Books.

24 10 reasons not to hit your child. (2020). Ask Dr Sears. Retrieved from http://askdrsears.com/topics/parenting/discipline-behavior/spanking/10-reasons-not-hit-your-child

25 Rhodes, M. (2017, October 2). When children begin to lie, there's actually a positive takeaway. *NPR.* Retrieved from https://www.npr.org/sections/13.7/2017/10/02/552860553/when-children-begin-to-lie-theres-actually-a-positive-takeaway

26 Lefkowitz, E. S., & Stoppa, T. M. (2006). Positive sexual communication and socialization in the parent-adolescent context. *New Directions for Child and Adolescent Development, 112*, 39-55.

27 Kirby, D., & Brent C. Miller, B. C. (2002). Interventions designed to promote parent-teen communication about sexuality. *New Directions for Child and Adolescent Development, 97*, 93-110.

28 Suleiman, A. B., Galván, A., Harden, K. P., & Dahl, R. E. (2017). Becoming a sexual being: The 'elephant in the room' of adolescent brain development. *Developmental Cognitive Neuroscience, 25*, 209-220.

29 Suleiman, A. B., Galván, A., Harden, K. P., & Dahl, R. E. (2017). Becoming a sexual being: The 'elephant in the room' of adolescent brain development. *Developmental Cognitive Neuroscience, 25*, 209-220.

30 Arbeit, M. R. (2014). What does healthy sex look like among youth? Towards a skills-based model for promoting adolescent sexuality development. *Human Development, 57*, 259-286.

31 Arbeit, M. R. (2014). What does healthy sex look like among youth? Towards a skills-based model for promoting adolescent sexuality development. *Human Development, 57*, 259-286.

32   Shtarkshall, R. A., Santelli, J. S., & Hirsch, J. S. (2007). Sex education and sexual socialization: Roles for educators and parents. *Perspectives on Sexual and Reproductive Health, 39*(2), 116-119.

33   Arbeit, M. R. (2014). What does healthy sex look like among youth? Towards a skills-based model for promoting adolescent sexuality development. *Human Development, 57,* 259-286.

34   Hedin, D., Hannes, K., & Saito, R. (1985). Minnesota youth poll: Youth look at themselves and the world, *AD-MR-Agricultural Experiment Station, University of Minnesota.*

35   Hare, B., & Woods, V. (2020). *Survival of the friendliest: Understanding our origins and rediscovering our common humanity.* New York: Random House.

36   The 4 most important types of exercise. (2023, August 8). *Harvard Health Pubishing, Harvard Medical School.* Retrieved from https://www.health.harvard.edu/exercise-and-fitness/the-4-most-important-types-of-exercise

37   Benefits of physical activity. (2023, August 1). *Centers for Disease Control and Prevention.* Retrieved from https://www.cdc.gov/physicalactivity/basics/pa-health/

38   U.S. Department of Health and Human Services. (2018). *Physical activity guidelines for Americans, 2nd edition.* Department of Health and Human Services: Washington, DC. Retrieved from https://health.gov/sites/default/files/2019-09/Physical_Activity_Guidelines_2nd_edition.pdf

39   Plata, M. (2018, October 31). How to spot your emotional triggers. *Psychology Today.* Retrieved from https://www.psychologytoday.com/us/blog/the-gen-y-psy/201810/how-spot-your-emotional-triggers

40   Reynolds, M. (2015, July 8). 5 steps for managing your emotional triggers. *Psychology.* Retrieved from https://www.psychologytoday.com/us/blog/wander-woman/201507/5-steps-managing-your-emotional-triggers

41   Plata, M. (2018, October 31). How to spot your emotional triggers. *Psychology Today.* Retrieved from https://www.psychologytoday.com/us/blog/the-gen-y-psy/201810/how-spot-your-emotional-triggers

42   Raypole, C. (2020, November 13). How to identify and manage your emotional triggers. *Healthline.* Retrieved from https://www.healthline.com/health/mental-health/emotional-triggers

43   Cognitive behavioral therapy. (2019, March 16). *Mayo Clinic.* Retrieved from https://www.mayoclinic.org/tests-procedures/cognitive-behavioral-therapy/about/pac-20384610

44   Azar, S. T., Reitz, E. B., & Goslin, M. C. (2008). Mothering: Thinking is part of the job description: Application of cognitive views to understanding maladaptive parenting and doing intervention and prevention work. *Journal of Applied Development Psychology, 29,* 295-304.

45   Powell, A. (2018). When science meets mindfulness. *The Harvard Gazette.* Retrieved from: https://news.harvard.edu/gazette/story/2018/04/harvard-researchers-study-how-mindfulness-may-change-the-brain-in-depressed-patients/

46   Valente, V., & Marotta, A. (2005). The impact of yoga on the professional and personal life of the psychotherapist. *Contemporary Family Therapy, 27*(1), 65-80.

47   Frazier, J. (2012). *Freedom of being: At ease with what is.* San Francisco, CA: Weiser Books.

48   National Center for Education Statistics. (2021). *Table 233.30: Number of students upended and expelled from public elementary and secondary schools, by sex, race/ethnicity, and state: 2017-18.* Retrieved from https://nces.ed.gov/programs/digest/d21/tables/dt21_233.30.asp